In a world of busy bodies and busy hearts, Kristen does a masterful job guiding us back to the source of our rest—God's inspired prayer book for all times, all places, all situations, and all people types—that we know as the Psalms. Perhaps there is no more relevant time than now to reacquaint ourselves with these inspired, life-giving prayers. Thank you, Kristen, for putting a spotlight on a peace that's always been, and is ever still, ours for the asking.

Scott Sauls, senior pastor of Christ Presbyterian Church in Nashville, Tennessee and author of *Befriend* and *From Weakness to Strength*

In a world where chaos and struggles seem to await us around every corner, Kristen uses her beautifully penned words to point us to a God who is waiting for us to simply rest in Him. She points us to the one who calms our souls and shows up in our lives when we least expect it. You will cry in this book, you will laugh in this book, and you will smile while reading, but most of all, you will see a God who sees His children. You will read about a God who cares about His children and cares about you. You will feel loved while reading this book.

Jamie Ivey, host of the podcast *The Happy Hour with Jamie Ivey*, and author of *If You Only Knew*

At the end of the day, so many of us are searching for the same thing: peace. The search itself can be one of dissonant struggle when we wrestle and stress and exhaustedly strive to untangle all that stands in our way. In *Finding Selah*, Kristen Kill is a most empathetic and understanding guide in the journey to a peaceful spirit. Alongside this tender and gracious friend, we discover that peace isn't so much a state of being to achieve, as it is embodied most fully in a person named Jesus.

Logan Wolfram, author of *Curious Faith*, speaker, and host/CEO of the Allume Conference

Finding Selah meets us right in middle of our hurried, harried, scheduled, and striving lives, and woos us to the kind of rest that doesn't require change in location or change in circumstances. Kristen shows us how peace and rest is found in receiving from God in the mundane, the chaos, the heartaches, and in everyday moments we might otherwise miss Him. Eyes that see, ears that listen, and hearts redirected—that's the path to rest *Finding Selah* offers.

Ruth Chou Simons, mom of 6, artist, bestselling author of *GraceLaced*, and founder of GraceLaced.com

Beautifully woven with grace and truth, *Finding Selah* extends a gentle invitation to hold on to hope when we're feeling weary and discover the peace that comes when our daily rhythms are rooted in Him.

Ruth Schwenk, coauthor of *Pressing Pause and* founder of TheBetterMom.com

"Selah" is God reaching out to every woman's heart with the pause we long for and somehow sense we're missing, whether we know it or not. The invitation to rest and be still—to be guilt-free—is one that every mom needs to receive again and again in the midst of a world whose every refrain is "more more more, louder louder louder!" In *Finding Selah*, Kristen gently walks us through the process of being vulnerable with God through joy and heartache, allowing Him to sing over and refresh us with His love and approval.

Jamie C. Martin, author of *Give Your Child the World* and cofounder of SimpleHomeschool.net

"These pages, they sing. In our cacophony of a world, Kristin Kill gently, artfully, and masterfully invites us back to the quiet of Him. I'll gift this book, over and over again."

Sara Hagerty, author of *Every Bitter Thing is Sweet* and *Unseen*

"After reading *Finding Selah*, I just exhaled. With beautiful, life-giving, artful words, Kristen unfolds a story and a hope for all of us who are desperate to breathe and find rest in the middle of our overwhelm. *Finding Selah* is a book to savor."

Sarah Mae, coauthor of *Desperate: Hope for the Mom Who Needs to Breathe*

Kristen cares about the heart of women, and she cares about the heart of God. This is so incredibly evident in her book, and you'll be blessed to slow down, settle in, and find *selah* in her words and in His Word. You'll be so thankful you read this, and you'll want to pass it around your friend group or buy one for all the gals you know. Thanks, Kristen, for leading the women of our generation so beautifully!

Jess Connolly, coauthor of *Wild and Free*
and author of *Dance, Stand, Run*

Beautifully written and masterfully woven together, *Finding Selah* is chock-full of soul-stirring stories and truth that surrounds the reader in a peaceful, restful way. Even the most stressed, desperate, and overwhelmed will find respite between each of the words that Kristen Kill writes. *Finding Selah* offers a soothing and calming encounter that will forever change even the most restless and reminds all of us that knowing God and His peace makes all the difference in the way we live in the world.

Chrystal Evans Hurst, author of *She's Still There*

Crazy busy is a feeling I think most, if not all, of us are well aquatinted with. No matter what season of life we are in, our days can feel so hurried and hectic. Maybe it's even fair to say we feel like we've been taken hostage to our frenzied schedules, and no matter how hard we try, we can't attain the peace we crave. Or we do find it, but it all too quickly slips through our busy hands. This is why I'm so grateful for the inspired words my friend Kristen Kill has penned in *Finding Selah*. Kristen shows us how doing life in a new rhythm—a rhythm of rest that is anchored in grace—is not only possible but promised to those who accept God's invitation to daily intimacy with Him.

Jeannie Cunnion, author of *Mom Set Free*

finding selah

THE SIMPLE PRACTICE OF PEACE WHEN YOU NEED IT MOST

KRISTEN KILL

ZONDERVAN

Finding Selah

Requests for information should be addressed to:
Zondervan, *3900 Sparks Dr. SE, Grand Rapids, Michigan 49546*

ISBN 978-0-310-34706-4 (audio)

ISBN 978-0-310-34702-6 (ebook)

Library of Congress Cataloging-in-Publication Data

Names: Kill, Kristen, author.
Title: Finding selah : the simple practice of peace when you need it most / Kristen Kill.
Description: Grand Rapids, Michigan : Zondervan, [2018] | Includes bibliographical references.
Identifiers: LCCN 2017033402 | ISBN 9780310347699 (softcover)
Subjects: LCSH: Peace of mind—Religious aspects—Christianity. | Christian life.
Classification: LCC BV4908.5 .K55 2018 | DDC 248.4—dc23 LC record available at https://lccn.loc.gov/2017033402

Published in association with the Literary Agency of D.C. Jacobson & Associates LLC, an Author Management Company www.dcjacobson.com.

Art direction: Tim Green | Faceout Studio
Interior design: Denise Froehlich

First printing November 2017 / Printed in the United States of America

For Josh
and for our beautiful children,
Halle, Maia, Jones, Lael, and Harris
May the song of heaven always stir your hearts most.

Contents

Foreword

I remember how the sunset shadows danced through the window in my Colorado home as I took my seat next to a guest I did not know yet. I was feeling shy, not finding much in my brain to say except, "Isn't the sunset over the mountains breathtaking?"

Perhaps it was a foreshadowing of our deep friendship to come. Darkness and light mingling together, golden dancing through the moments, as if to defy the darkness, giving a memorable performance to mark our first meeting.

I had invited fifty women into my home for a long weekend to mentor them in the ways of loving Jesus, and I had met only a handful of them.

Introverted at heart but passionate in spirit, I was comfortable speaking to thousands but shy in a smaller group where I had to make chit-chatty conversation. When I sat down next to Kristen, I did not know that she would become one of my dearest friends. But I did feel relief that she smiled at me, welcomed me with her deep, penetrating eyes, and said, "I was hoping you would sit here."

Over the next years, I visited Kristen in her tiny New York apartment when I visited my son, who was living there. She attended events in my Colorado home and joined me at conferences, small groups, in multiple settings across the US. I began to realize that when I was with Kristen, I could share my deepest thoughts, my feelings of failure, my desires to quit ministry from time to time because of being overwhelmed.

I always knew that when we spent time together, I would leave feeling deeply loved and accepted for who I was, even though she knew my faults. Giggling together over silly moments, drinking gallons of coffee together, speaking of every aspect of life from lipstick to raising godly children, I realized that I had a treasure in a friend like her. Not only did she make me feel loved as I was, but she always called me to be my best self. I found in her solace for my anxious thoughts, affirmation for my ideals, and passion for God that always made me want to be more faithful, more willing to walk in His love.

As I came to know Kristen deeply, I understood that she had walked through many dark nights in her own personal story. Yet like the golden light dancing the first evening I met her, she always found a way to sparkle, to find light, to trust God, to learn from the deep hurts and struggles in her life. From these daunting places, she learned to sympathize with and create refuge for others who also walked in dark places but needed to find light amidst their darkness. She extends peace through the storms and a contagious love for a heavenly Father who will walk with her each step until she sees Him face to face.

As you read her words, you will find a friend who welcomes you, an empathetic companion who understands struggles and failures, someone who inspires you to dance while choosing to find joy, and an advocate who gives you the grace to find rest, hope, and peace in your own journey.

Thank you, sweet Kristen, for walking with me, loving me, and helping me to find *selah* in all the moments of my life.

Sally Clarkson

CHAPTER 1

From Silence to Symphony

With the psalms, we bring into awareness an ancient sorry release, a latent joy. We use the psalms to present ourselves before God as honestly as we are able.

EUGENE PETERSON, *PSALMS, PRAYERS OF THE HEART*

The silence terrified me most in those early days of motherhood.

I was such a young mama, not quite twenty-two, married for only a little more than a year when nurses and midwives placed my first baby girl onto my chest. I snuggled her close as she quivered, chilled. Halle was slick with waxy goo, and my lips had barely kissed her bald, balmy head before the medical team covered her with a tiny cap and warm blankets. I enveloped her in my arms, and it felt like she'd always belonged there. It came naturally to me to comfort her, to try to ease her surprise at being ripped from her calm existence in my cozy womb. In those first moments with a baby, it's all cooing and shushing sounds and rocking in an attempt to woo them to their new world. There is no way to rationalize or whisper to an infant about the wonder to come, no way to express anticipation for the sights, smells, tastes, and love that awaits them. A swaddled infant will never understand that one day soon they will actually long to spread their arms *wide*. And so we rock and soothe and swaddle.

It's funny how we hush our children to offer comfort, isn't it? There is an invitation in being still when we are trying to console our babies, when we are making room for them to feel or adjust. That kind of silence is a soft, patient embrace.

But the silence that followed in my days as a new mom—the silence I feared—was the kind that rings and pulses in your ears. All alone and unseen, retreating and overwhelmed, I chose to hide as my seemingly perfect life began to crumble.

A Blush Pink Beginning

My husband and I met when we were still undergrads. Josh wore glasses and had a singular dimple. His smile lit up his eyes and my heart in turn. We lived in different countries that first year; he was at university, and I was at a discipleship training school in Hawaii and then working as a missionary in Thailand. We exchanged long letters and emails, scattering our souls in all those words, in all the honest hopes we could share freely with the buffer of an ocean between us. One night, as I sat with my ear pressed to a payphone, palms swaying around me, Josh started talking about marriage and our future. I knew then that when I flew home, we would knit a life together. Not long after that, when I was only twenty, I looped my arm through my dad's and squeezed tightly as we glided down the aisle to the tune of a fairy tale. My wedding was all Martha Stewart, back when her magazine was fresh and people had just realized they could have customized wedding invitations. The bridesmaids wore blush pink, and the men wore morning jackets for a noon affair. The afternoon reception was a swirl of soft lighting and cream-colored fondant. I had no idea at the time that fondant is actually a little sticky to the touch and tastes like stale marshmallows; I just knew it was what magazines featured on wedding cakes, and I wanted it.

I approached much of our life as newlyweds the way I chose my wedding cake. I didn't anticipate anything sticky or unpleasant; I just wanted all the pretty. And in the beginning, life was smooth and sweet. We lived in a picturesque university town an hour north of Seattle and just thirty minutes from the Canadian border, situated on a beautiful bay of Puget Sound. We both studied. I decorated. I carefully chose the theme of our first Christmas tree. (*Martha Stewart Living* magazine was, of course, consulted at length.) It was full of copper and gold, with magenta ribbons and emerald accents. It matched our hunter green chair, and I remember sitting and staring at it every night, thinking about how it felt like magic. I found I loved to host Bible studies and dinner parties, and I also learned to cook, to marinate and bake and present side dishes. I think I squealed when we took a bite of my first roast, it was that good. I'd never thought I could make a dish like that, and there we were, eating it with potatoes and carrots that had been roasted in a beautiful terra cotta pan.

We read a lot in those early days. It was more like inhaling books together, lobbing ideas across the dinner table, getting lost in conversations over candlelight. Sometimes we donned headlamps and explored tide pools of the Pacific when the water sank low in the middle of the night. Sometimes we camped or hiked or took long drives up into the mountains. We explored the urban center of Vancouver. I imagined our life together would go on like this forever. Studying would stretch into the work of new careers, and we'd collect adventures the way I collected index cards for my recipe box.

Then, all of a sudden I couldn't stop throwing up. I felt weak most mornings. I couldn't miss class, I told myself; I had to keep pushing through. Then I passed out in the chemistry lab. In dramatic fashion, following an ambulance ride and a couple of tests, we found out we were having a baby. First came the shock, followed by all sorts of creative budgeting and number crunching but mostly a whole lot of delight. The week we learned we were going to be parents, a family sat in front of us at church with their baby girl, and I couldn't stop looking at the folds of her tiny wrists. She gripped her mother tightly, twisted her fingers through her hair, and played peek-a-boo shyly with us. Baby talking in return, I wished I could squeeze her. I realized then that I could hardly wait to experience the snuggle of my own baby, to hold her plump little hands and hear her giggle.

That semester, I had arranged to sit for my final exams early to make sure they were behind me before I went into labor. A passionate art history student, I couldn't put down my texts about the Parthenon and porticos, columns and cloisters, not even in my final trimester. I'd been reading about architecture the morning the contractions began tightening my belly. I took in air in calculated rhythms, deep and measured, timed by the second hand of the clock on the wall. With every inhale, with every swell of tension, I let my mind wander toward the marble and sandstone described in the pages still laid out on my coffee table. I distracted myself by imagining a walk through the gardens and under the archways of grand places of another time.

I was transported when I first held my baby girl on my chest. Time stopped. The midwives whirled around my daughter as she woke to her birth. I lay perfectly still, hushed and hesitant to move. The weight of welcoming this child seemed to require a sort of reverence. In the reception of a new soul, heaven met us, flooding the space with repose, even as medical instruments clanged and beeped and buzzed around us.

I looked at the nurses scurrying around with blankets and monitors and proud gazes. They had ushered in a new life, but did they know they had helped to birth something new inside of me too? I was both undone and remade in those first moments of motherhood, all at once. The early days of any unfamiliar season always grip us uniquely as our senses rise to something new, and I was aware of every breath. I wanted nothing more than to embrace each moment completely, with focus and endearment.

A Disquieting Hush

I'm not sure when I lost my footing, when the silence turned from gorgeous gift to burden to bear. New motherhood can surely make anyone spin, but I didn't seem to be able to stop the spiral—at least not without falling over. It became hard to dress each day, to accomplish simple tasks. My productivity waned, but internally my mind was on a tear. I woke most nights in a sweat, worried my baby wasn't breathing and urgently rushing to the crib to check on her. I obsessed about how she nursed, if she was meeting every milestone, and if I was doing enough. *Was I?* Our cozy home was filled with new index cards, scrawled with instructions to myself about what to clean, how to cook, where to be. Everything had to be calculated. If I veered too far from my plan, anxiety gripped me. I was running ragged. My own thoughts were an echo chamber whispering that I would never get any of it right.

Josh and I stared at one another across the table in the evenings, and I knew my eyes were dull, that some of the light had gone from them. I was mechanical and unfeeling, just inserting reactions and smiles and nods where they seemed appropriate. "Hmmmm . . . Yes . . . Definitely." Then *smile*. My personality was slipping away in a postpartum fog, and I didn't know how to connect with anyone. I worried that if I did reach out, they'd discover I was reeling inside, that my heart was in shambles. So I listened serenely, fooling everyone (I thought) as I baked cupcakes and hosted playgroups, always playing a part.

When I faced myself alone, there was no hiding. I'd open my journal, and even my pen lay immobile. I cried out for God to draw near, to give me words to pray, but my voice was parched.

This season was a paradox. My emotions were an array of sadness and confusion, but I had never imagined such love and tenderness could exist. I wanted those small moments to stretch into thousands more like them and make my life a constellation glowing with wild love. With my face nuzzled into my girl's newborn head, I'd sway, basking in the scent that all new mothers know by heart: fresh skin, a whiff of baby shampoo and soft laundry soap. As I kissed my way down her forehead to reach her tiny cheeks, her breath came in a sleepy rhythm matching the rise and fall of her tummy. I'd sing her name softly—*Halle girl, my Halle girl*—and she'd smile to welcome rest, her eyes closing, lashes aflutter. How could I hold this holy gift, be so completely satisfied in caring for her, and also be so severely plagued by loneliness, by isolation, by fear and by doubt? I felt utterly in love and utterly trapped, and any rumbling of the disharmony straining my heart was muffled by the silence. Hollow, aching silence.

I wondered, too, how to justify the cadence of my days at home. They felt slow, tedious, insignificant. I'd never experienced such an expanse of time to cultivate anything, and yet I couldn't muster productivity, let alone creativity. I had dreamed of this season, and somehow I had still become what I saw as a cliché: the new mother, undone, still in pajamas at five o'clock, unable to even shower. Hours were spent shushing and patting, striving, willing with all my might for my daughter to fall asleep as I paced up and down the hall.

That's where I caught the reflection of my wide eyes and chalky skin—a face I didn't know starred back at me in the entryway mirror. I didn't recognize my own face. I knew I was letting myself sink into emotions that were much larger than I was. I was withdrawn, avoiding a silence of my own making, afraid to ask for help and worried that my weakness made me unfit.

Years later, when I had my other children, the world was already different. Postpartum depression had earned a household name and people were more open to talking about taking medication to heal from it, in the same way we used to talk about taking Tylenol. Even routine pediatric visits included screenings for new moms: *Do you find yourself crying often? Are you able to enjoy things as much as you always have? Do you have fears about your baby's safety?* But when I had Halle, depression in new mothers was fringe theory. The advice of most doctors was to get fresh air, take long walks, and try to sleep when the baby finally closed her eyes. These are all good things, but they are not solutions for a brain on fire and hormones that refuse to stabilize. So many women like me were left alone as we tangled ourselves up, trying everything we knew to care for our minds and bodies, to counter the stresses of sleep deprivation and anxiety and the nagging feeling that we weren't doing enough.

Through it all, God and I spoke less and less. I continued to falter in prayer. Sometimes I could hear His voice, but it was no longer a melody in my heart.

Instead, I'd begun to become comfortable a different, more chaotic tempo. I filled my calendar with endless activity, never allowing myself time to slow. I tried to secure for myself days when the silence couldn't catch me, days when I'd never have to be alone.

How many of my sisters have felt the burden of overloaded days and then wondered where all their time has gone? How many of us sway to the beat of busyness, only to find ourselves out of step and panting for breath? We can so easily ache for peace even as we fear what we will hear if we are truly quiet. Restless, we wear the weight of work, of performance, of expectations, of our own distractions or addictions. And before we know it, we are living in discord.

Searching for a Symphony

When I was sixteen, I traveled to Europe on a student exchange. One evening, I tiptoed into an alabaster concert hall, just blocks away from the birthplace of Mozart, with a group of friends from my high school. As kids from the New World, we were already mesmerized by the land we found ourselves in, our senses absorbing every detail. As we entered the room where the concert would be performed that night, I was struck by the contrast of its grandeur and its commonality. Perhaps this is always the experience when one visits an old city for the first time, keenly aware of history and modern-day details joined in one place. The arched floor-to-ceiling windows stretched along one wall, and just beyond them, the daily produce market tents and evening shoppers bustled to buy carrots and apples and greens. Baroque details and inlaid carvings lined the window frames and doorways. Some of the molding sparkled and fanned out in shapes painted in enamel hues of pink and gold. The center of the room was lined with wooden chairs, the type you might find at a garden wedding anywhere in the world, and near the front were more chairs still, arranged in a half moon with a music stand set before each one. This is where the musicians would be: not on a stage or platform at a high distance, and not hidden in an orchestra pit beneath a theatre, but right before us, *among us*. It felt *intimate*.

When they entered and began to tune their strings, a familiar cacophony reverberated along the arches and across the stone tiles. For the moment, they were tuned to themselves, consumed only by the instrument they held in their hands, wielding them, twisting them into position for the song to come, yet they were woefully out of sync with every other performer on the floor.

The grand mystery of making music is that there is a point during every performance when all the bedlam becomes a tune, when those scratches on each page align the tones into a song. Each note becomes an ally of the next, and clamor gives way to music.

Again and again, the tune rings out in halls just like this, along the walls and windows of a room that held the masters, that welcomed Mozart as a neighbor boy, and later, welcomed even me. The music transcends time and structure, never losing its ability to awaken the human heart.

I think we are all drawn to a symphony. We long for rhythms and tempos to turn chaos into something sublime, for all the disjointed players and pieces of our lives to culminate in a perfect melody. We desperately want things to work out, to work together, to produce beauty. And while we wait for the notes to find their places, we accept the dissonance. Jangled and discontented, we hear only clanging noise, even as we hold out hope for harmony. *At least it's a sound,* we think. *At least there isn't silence.* Because that would feel hopeless . . . wouldn't it?

The Soul of Words

Near our apartment, a cafe with cold stone walls nestled inside a bookstore. I'd often walk there with Halle when she was just a few months old to sip tea and get lost in the pages of stories. It was an oasis in the bleary days when I felt alone, plus the cafe made the most delicious chicken pie, with perfectly stewy insides and a flaky crust. I'd sit for long spans of time while the baby napped and let the gravy warm my soul while I licked the spoon. One evening, while I sopped up a small feast and read and cooed to my girl, a poet rose and began a reading. There were just a few of us gathered near him, and I think my first response was to roll my eyes. Living in a progressive college town meant the parameters of art were loosely defined, always nudging the line of convention. But as the words began to slip from his lips, clearly spilling from his heart, my senses awakened. I *had* to listen, I had to hear the way he conducted speech like music—like a symphony.

Poetry is *root* language. It is emotive; it holds the soul of words. As I listened to this poet, mesmerized more by the sound of his prose than its substance, I was reminded that Scripture, too, contains poetry—poetry I hadn't read for quite some time. The psalms are where the poetry is found in the Bible. Like all poems, they find their form *beneath* their verses. Poetry reaches beyond words to communicate to our senses, to annotate every emotion. As Eugene Peterson wrote, "The poetry of the Psalms required that we deal with our actual humanity, these worlds dive beneath the surfaces of prose and pretense straight into the depths."[1]

My walk home was crisp and quick, marked by a sense of urgency to open my Bible and read those emotive prayers again, this time with my whole heart. As I flipped through the thin pages, I realized just how long it had been since I'd last done so. My heart was racing, full of hope.

There, in the psalms, I was met with the words and prayers of saints who had cried out to God in the midst of their own pain. They had sung . . .

> My life is consumed by anguish
>   and my years by groaning;
> my strength fails because of my affliction,
>   and my bones grow weak.
>
> PSALM 31:10

> My bones suffer mortal agony
>   as my foes taunt me,
> saying to me all day long,
>   "Where is your God?"

Why, my soul, are you downcast?
Why so disturbed within me?

PSALM 42:10–11

I am worn out from my groaning.
All night long I flood my bed with weeping
and drench my couch with tears.
My eyes grow weak with sorrow.

PSALM 6:6–7

I was not alone. The psalmists had cried too; they had felt emotions that were big and loud and desperate. They prayed visceral, honest, intimate prayers. And you know what I realized? It made me uncomfortable. When they worried that their circumstances might swallow them up, they had not withdrawn; instead, they had *drawn close*. And I was doing the opposite, tiptoeing before God, both afraid of the silence and afraid to speak. I was terrified to choose stillness and face the empty quiet within. But our stillness guides our knowing. Silence opens our hearts to heaven.

In our ceasing, we *see*.

The Lord whispers, "Be still . . ."

He instructs us with a promise and with an invitation to see Him:

"Be still and know that I am God."[2]
"Stand firm and see the salvation of the Lord."[3]

There is a silence that heralds knowing God. One prepares the way for the other. Even as I struggled to trust God with the storm inside me, I read about how He calms the waters. And from that stillness emerged a new song, or rather, a psalm:

> [You] who stilled the roaring of the seas, the roaring of their waves, and the turmoil of the nations. The whole earth is filled with awe at your wonders, where morning dawns, where evening fades, you call forth songs of Joy.[4]

My eyes hovered over the words and I straightened. *Could you call forth a song of joy in me, Jesus? Bring a melody out of my discord? Could I embrace the promise that music would fill my life, like it filled that concert hall with strings so many years ago? Could my life become a psalm?*

It was the first time I had tried to talk to God in months. Whisper by whisper, prayer by small prayer, I began to return, to trust that God was there, to cling to His promise that in stillness He would be made known. Have you ever blundered through a reunion, not sure how to approach an old friend or where to begin to fill the gaps since your last conversation? There are often clumsy pauses, polite apologies, and in my case, a tendency to get off rhythm in the back and forth of listening and speaking. Returning to prayer after a long time felt like that. I'd forgotten *how* to pray, how to let go of all I was carrying. There was so much that burdened and crowded my heart. I didn't know how to begin to express it all. As I began to try to pour out my anxiety, my depression, and even my doubt before God, I simply sighed. *Help. Help my unbelief.*

Sometimes the shortest prayers spoken with great faith are those that change our lives the most. Just plain and true. *Help.* My eyes scanned the pages of the psalms again, and I began to read the words not as those of someone else, but as my own cry, my own heart, my own prayer to God. The same verse from Psalm 6 was different in my voice:

I am worn out from my groaning.

Lord, I am so worn and so many places in my life feel thin and threadbare. I feel tired and tread upon, and something is crying out from within me. A grumble, a lament, a grief I can't name, but it is wearing on me always . . .

All night long I flood my bed with weeping and drench my couch with tears.

Lord, this child you have given me, oh, how I love her, but my tears never stop. I am crying day and night, my eyes swollen, my emotions running wild. My body and mind do not feel like my own. I am so tired and so afraid.

My eyes grow weak with sorrow.

Lord, how long can I keep going? I am so weary, but can I stop? How can I lay down these activities, these roles for which others count on me? How can I ever rest when there is so much that needs to be done?

There was no posturing or posing as I read God's word as prayer. In the days and weeks that followed, it began to give form to my emotions and helped me carry them, little by little, back home to Him. With each outcry, each moment of suffering, or even of jubilation and praise, I was finding the curve of my own heart within the psalmist's stanzas, drawing close, *knowing* God, softening into the stillness.

CHAPTER 2

The Hardest Part

He was singing a melody he did not know, and yet the notes poured from his throat with all the assurance of long familiarity . . . as long as the ancient harmonies were sung, the Universe would not entirely lose its joy.

MADELINE L'ENGLE, *A SWIFTLY TILTING PLANET*

"You are so angry. I think you are holding it tight, like this, right in the stomach."

As Ana formed the words in broken English, she squeezed her hands into fists, drawing them to her waist.

"The anger is stuck right there."

I barely knew this woman. My interactions with her had been brief and often unpleasant. We spoke different languages, and we were separated even further by cultural differences.

Josh had finished college, and we were spending the year in Bavaria as missionaries. He was taking Biblical Studies classes, and we were both part of local and international outreach efforts. Halle was nearly two, and as a young mother and an adjunct to the work and studies of my husband, I was consumed by exploring the area with my little girl, visiting local shops and taking long walks in the village below the fourteenth century hunting castle that was our home. We'd walk and buy strudel and visit the cows in the barn before returning for Halle's nap. This lull in my day provided the opportunity to invite students in for heart-to-hearts over tea. We'd pass the pastries and our whole hearts around the table.

My strengths were relational while Ana took a more task-oriented approach. She was brisk, direct, and sharp. It was her job to assign errands and chores for students and staff to keep our missionary base running smoothly. She frequently barked instructions and made no effort to conceal her frustration when they weren't carried out with efficiency and precision. I often felt as though I was in her way.

As she confronted me, I couldn't help wondering, who was Ana to think *I* was angry? Wasn't I intentionally playful and gentle, a doting mother, a loving wife? I tried hard. If either of us was angry, surely it was her. She was severe even now as she sat before me, a scowl permanently stamped on her brow.

We'd been randomly paired together to pray during a worship service. Specifically, we were instructed to seek and ask God what areas of our lives He wanted to heal. Ana didn't know me; it was simple chance that we were sitting together, but God knew I needed to receive the words she expressed, to hear them from someone I assumed embodied the very ache that throbbed within me.

But as she spoke, I realized my indignation was not with Ana; it was with the truth revealed in her assessment of me. She saw through my mask, saw behind my carefully constructed facade. She was right; I sensed something in my gut, simmering like a poison, eating away at me and sometimes seeping out.

Ana's voice drifted as her eyes welled with unexpected tears. She unfurled her fist and stretched out her hand to take mine. In my discomfort, I diverted my gaze toward my toddler playing a few feet away. My inclination was to ignore her words, to tend to my daughter, to carry on, to keep concealing and stay safely in denial. I was afraid to look her in the eye and be seen any further. I wanted to run away. To stay silent and avoid her. My cheeks burned, and I felt woozy. I felt exposed and confronted and nervous, but most of all numb. Our encounter was the first honest conversation I'd had with anyone except Josh in a long time, and there was no faking it. I knew Ana saw the real me. And somehow, not in spite of who I was, but *because* of all my shortcomings, she extended kindness and invited me to be her friend. There was the hope of relief, as if the most unlikely of friends was greeting me on the road, pointing the way toward home.

There was something both terrifying and freeing about being really seen by someone else and finding I was accepted. Even though the tangles of my heart and mind were finding a name and a form as I prayed the psalms, there were pieces of myself I would have preferred to shoosh away and keep unseen and unknown and certainly unknown, characteristics deep in my soul of living in a fallen place. But stuffing away the hardest parts—shame, control, fear and doubt—meant that those things were swelling together and beginning to fester within me.

In the body, five minutes of anger can shut down the immune system for approximately six hours. Just *five minutes*. That's all it takes to neutralize your physical ability to defend your body from disease and illness. Can you imagine what happens when anger is allowed to smolder? Can you envision what festers beneath stored resentment and bitterness, below the dark, toxic emotions we can hold deep inside?

Researchers tell us that over time, anger triggers an adrenal response that leads to an increase in stress, heart disease, the risk of stroke, headaches, and insomnia. Anger causes your muscles and your very life to contract. They tighten up and harden right along with our hearts. When you're angry, your stomach literally shunts blood to your muscles. It transforms from a smooth, vulnerable organ into tougher, striated tissue that easily constricts. Anger moves us from softness to hardness, from fragile to flinching. The Oxford English Dictionary says the word *shunt*, apart from describing a change of course, comes from the word *shonen*, in Middle English, and means to hide, or evade.[1]

No wonder God repeatedly instructs His people to put off anger, warning of the way it overwhelms and brings strife. When we take it on and take it in, the tension lodges deep, takes hold, twists and clutches inside us, distorting our affections and feelings. The anger simmering in me was the root of my own disguise and shame.

In the book of Mark, we see one of the few instances in Scripture where Jesus becomes *angry*. It's an interesting passage because in it, we observe both the anger of Christ, the kind of anger that's bred of righteousness, and the anger of the Pharisees, the kind of anger that hardens hearts and grieves God. As Jesus enters the synagogue on the Sabbath, the Pharisees are watching Him, looking to accuse Him of breaking religious law. They are on the prowl, and right in front of them, Jesus approaches a man whose hand is withered and worn. Jesus is about to make him new, to heal him with the touch of heaven, but he's also going to show us something even greater: His forgiveness, the grace that changes everything about a person.

As He approaches the man, He directs His attention toward the Pharisees, and asks, "Is it lawful on the Sabbath to do good or to do harm, to save life or to kill?"[2] And then He tells the man with shriveled bone and muscle to stretch out his hand, and it is restored. The Pharisees, we are told, were filled with *fury*, and Jesus was *angered* by their hardness of heart. He was grieved at what escaped them: *truth, healing, softness*. He was grieved that in their anger, they evaded his love. The reality of God Himself in their midst eluded them; they missed Him, along with the possibility of their own restoration and flourishing. They missed Him because they were too consumed with hiding themselves, too concerned with being right, too hard.

In my own hiding, and my own obsession with being perfect, I'd become hardened and unfeeling, just like the Pharisees. I'd begun to express the depths of my heart before God, but now He was calling me to trust him with even more, with the darkest parts that I wanted to deny. And now Ana had called me out.

Why couldn't I be like the man with the dry bones, desperate at the door of the house of God? He had stretched out his hand, reaching for Jesus, and Christ had taken his flesh in His own palm, transformed what was atrophied and decaying, and restored it to life. Courageously, the man had cast off the expectations of the Law and all his ideas of how to live perfect. He chose instead to touch Jesus. To embrace Him above all else.

To those watching, this must have seemed a very odd choice. The Pharisees measured their worth by their *obedience* to the Law. Without Jesus, identity and self-worth are always about comparing and sizing up. We can get stuck seeking affirmation from those who like us or who *are* like us. We check to make sure we measure up, to assess whether our way is still best, to see if we should feel inferior or superior to others. How many times have I wished my home had more of a modern aesthetic after scrolling on the internet? Or that my girls all wore French braids at the beach, or that I could perfect hand lettering or bake a better birthday cake? Or, on the other hand, maybe I'm the one found shaking my head at a stranger feeding her babies fast food, judging fashion choices (Wide leg jeans are back? Tsk, tsk.) or smugly pointing out that, for the moment, my own children are not rolling their eyes at me like that other woman's kids over there. You see how easily we can begin to identify with what we see around us? How quick are we to find ourselves in relation to those around us or to how well we meet the standards we create in our minds?

When we wear religiosity in this way, we begin to believe we are saved because we are doing all the right things, following all the right rules, and little by little we try to *achieve* our wholeness and our holiness. In the process, we may not realize we have become more spiteful of everyone who is unlike us or that we slowly begin to exclude those who don't fit neatly into our camp.

Jesus was other. Different. He didn't abide by the patterns or plans of the Pharisees, and by breaking their rules, He called into question not only how they did things and what they deemed right, but their very selves, the identities they strove to craft. But where the Holy Spirit dwells, Hebrews tells us, the law is not simply rules but is alive and written on our hearts. And Jesus is its revealer:

> In the past God spoke to our ancestors through the prophets at many times and in various ways, but in these last days he

> has spoken to us by his Son, who he appointed heir of all things and through whom also he made the Universe.[3]

Jesus is the final word—the restorer of life, the softener of hearts, the revealer of *identity.* But you cannot be led by someone you do not *know.* To truly follow Jesus, to be healed by Jesus, means you must look Him in the face and know Him.

Here's the rub the Pharisees experienced: relationships, unlike an impersonal code of rules, have the ability to offend you and challenge you. They can make you uncomfortable and cause you to retreat—or to grow. The Pharisees chose offense. They chose a moral identity of works over the person of Christ. But the man who stretched out his hand? He was willing to risk it all to be with Jesus.

Was I?

As I prayed with Ana—a woman I'd previously criticized for not living by *my* rules—I had to decide if I wanted to be healed. If I would embrace Christ. I could remain hardened, I supposed, busy and blind to the anger creeping and crushing me from the inside, or I could reach out, returning the grip of a new friend. The gift of Ana's invitation was like a picture of the extension of God's own hand. I decided to embrace her in faith. In that moment, I was really embracing Christ, allowing Him to see me, to offend me and cause me to grow. I was willing to be known.

When Our Discord Is Covered in Feathers

[The joy in reaching out is found in knowing that the melody of God heals. It ties together all our sonatas and crescendos, all the cacophony into chorus. Life is not merely one bar followed] by another but sheets upon sheets of rhythm and refrain merging into a symphony. Even the silences play their part. Could I join the psalmists in both praise and lament with honesty? Their verses had been teaching me how to feel and to pray as a weary new mom, even with their brutality.

> I am poured out like water,
> and all my bones are out of joint.
> My heart has turned to wax;
> it has melted within me.
>
> My mouth is dried up like a potsherd,
> and my tongue sticks to the roof of my mouth;
> you lay me in the dust of death.

PSALM 22:14–15

> Listen, LORD, and answer me,
> for I am poor and needy.
> Protect my life, for I am faithful.
> You are my God; save Your servant who trusts in You.
> Be gracious to me, Lord,
> for I call to You all day long.
> Bring joy to Your servant's life,
> because I turn to You, Lord.

PSALM 86:1–4[4]

> We are brought down to the dust;
> our bodies cling to the ground.
> Rise up and help us;
> rescue us because of your unfailing love.

PSALM 44:25–26

> Restore us again, God our Savior,
> and put away your displeasure toward us.
> Will you be angry with us forever?
> Will you prolong your anger through all generations?
> Will you not revive us again,
> that your people may rejoice in you?
> Show us your unfailing love, LORD,
> and grant us your salvation.
>
> PSALM 85:4–7

I began to look even beyond this book. Job had cried out too. In his agony he wailed,

> I cry out to you, God, but you do not answer; I stand up, but you merely look at me. You turn on me ruthlessly; with the might of your hand you attack me. You snatch me up and drive me before the wind; you toss me about in the storm. I know you will bring me down to death, to the place appointed for all the living.[5]

Before my prayer time with Ana, I was struggling to share my deepest parts and my darkest hollows with God, with anyone. My prayers were often shallow. I settled for words that were pretty, that wouldn't irritate. But they were prayers that never revealed my true heart. Now I wanted him to know all of me. I was unwilling to let anger keep me at arm's length any longer. But I was still fearful. If I was honest, I wondered, how would God respond? Would I be rejected? Tossed out? Marked by all my doubt?

Because of our roots in the Pacific Northwest, friends across the country always ask us about a popular joke from the hit show

Portlandia, in which the Portlandians' strategy for making things cool is to simply "Put a bird on it." The phrase is now a meme associated with the city and has sparked a trend of putting birds on everything from t-shirts to tennis shoes. It's become another sweet reminder of one of my favorite creatures in nature. I've been birdwatching and reading Audubon books to my kids for years. I always put out little nests and blue robin's eggs around the house in the springtime. One of my favorite images of God in Scripture is Deuteronomy 32:11. The Lord is described as "an eagle that stirs up its nest, that flutters over its young, spreading out its wings, catching them; bearing them on its pinions."[6] All that is tender requires protection. Can you see the baby birds, fussed over by their mother fluttering about them? I ask myself, is this how I see God? I know that the vulnerable need a safe haven, and I know what it's like to flutter as a mom, accompanied by the coos and gurgles of a newborn. Their tendency is to nuzzle close, as they sleep, occasionally exhaling a deep, audible sigh. Babies are content and sheltered, completely at rest beside their mothers, tiny hands often clasping the soft edge of a sweater or gripping a finger tight. They turn toward us as they wake, searching until their eyes find ours. They brighten when we greet them with a smile and a soft voice. It's clear that babies know our delight. So small, even when they are brand new, they know the attention of their mothers is captivated by nothing more than their presence.

There was a time, however, when I stopped believing I was captivating the heart of God in such a way, even though He is clear about how He receives me and responds to me:

> He who dwells in the shelter of the Most High will rest in the shadow of the Almighty. I will say of the Lord, "He is

> my refuge and my fortress, my God, in whom I trust." Surely he will save you from the fowler's snare and from the deadly pestilence. He will cover you with his feathers and under his wings you will find refuge; his faithfulness will be your shield and rampart. You will not fear the terror of night, nor the arrow that flies by day, nor the pestilence that stalks in the darkness, nor the plague that destroys at midday. A thousand may fall at your side, ten thousand at your right hand, but it will not come near you. You will only observe with your eyes and see the punishment of the wicked. If you make the Most High Your dwelling—even the Lord, who is my refuge—then no harm will befall you, no disaster will come near your tent. For he will command his angels concerning you to guard you in all your ways; they will lift you up in their hands, so that you will not strike your foot against a stone. You will tread upon the lion and the cobra; you will trample the great lion and the serpent. "Because he loves me," says the Lord, "I will rescue him; I will protect him, for he acknowledges my name. He will call upon me, and I will answer him; I will protect him, for he acknowledges my name. He will call upon me, and I will answer him: I will be with him in trouble, I will deliver him and honor him. With long life will I satisfy him and show him my salvation.[7]

The Benson Commentary explains that this idea of being hidden under the wings of God, of dwelling in the shelter of the Lord, is even more extraordinary than we realize, that to rest in the shadow of the Almighty is referred to as "the most holy place in the tabernacle and temple, under the outstretched wings of the cherubim covering the ark and mercy-seat. It is as if the psalmist had said, 'He shall dwell like the ark in the holy of holies, under the immediate shadow and protection of the Divine Majesty.'"[8] As part of the Ark of the Covenant, the mercy seat was where God chose to *meet* His people; it was where His very presence dwelt. And the Lord says to the ones He loves, this is where *you* will be. Yes, you.

Discovering God's Song of Love

There are a few times in my life that feel like a photograph in my memory, like perfect pictures that have withstood time, and I can recall every detail of those moments.

I can remember right where I was when I first believed God delighted in me. I was immersed in the pines of Camp Firwood. I'd spent the whole summer working there among friends, my skin layered with dust and sweat by each day's end. Most evenings I bathed in the lake, taking a long dive off the dock after a lifeguarding shift before throwing on my fleece and joining the rest of camp for fireside songs. It was a summer that shaped my heart. I didn't know then how special it was to have those weeks away from my everyday world to rest, serve, and study God's Word. But one of the most pivotal moments was a quiet one alone on a cloudy morning. I left my bunk early to walk down the trail and sit on the dock for my morning devotions. Fog hung over the glassy surface of the lake, and I could hear an occasional plink as fish skimmed the top in search of breakfast. My hair was in its usual ponytail, my legs crisscrossed, my Bible open on my lap. I'd opened up Scripture at random, really. Hosea . . . Amos . . . Micah . . . Ah, Zephaniah. Yes, that would be the one. Three chapters. One book in one morning. So I began to read and then, chapter three, verse 17:

> The Lord your God is with you,
> the Mighty Warrior who saves.
> He will take great delight in you;
> in his love he will no longer rebuke you,
> but will rejoice over you with singing.

I read it again. The *Lord* is singing? Over me?

My entire identity was defined in these verses. The Lord delights in me. He is singing over me! I am his child.

I resisted at first. I'd focused so hard and so long on myself, on how I presented my heart, my life, my service, and my very worth before God and before others. But this was the first bud of truth that would blossom and grow throughout my life, even years later, until that moment with Ana when I was faced with all I held unsaid. I had to learn, and will always need to be reminded, that the spot where I begin, my starting point, is as one who is loved deeply by the God who spoke the stars into place.

This is where you begin too. Not as condemned but as beloved, delighted in, and covered by wings of protection and grace.

Did you know that the Scriptures say, "By the word of the Lord the heavens were made, their starry host by the *breath* of his mouth"?[9] The same breath exhaled life into mankind, awakening Adam from dust. One of my favorite accounts of creation is actually fictional, from *The Chronicles of Narnia*, the famous allegorical series by C. S. Lewis. In *The Magician's Nephew*, he describes the first awakening of Narnia:

> In the darkness something was happening at last. A voice had begun to sing . . . Sometime it seemed to come from all directions at once. Sometimes he almost thought was coming out

> of the earth beneath them. Its lower notes were deep enough to be the voice of the earth herself. There were no words. There was hardly even a tune. But it was, beyond comparison, the most beautiful noise he had ever heard . . . Then two wonders happened at the same moment. One was that the voice was suddenly joined by other voices; more voices than you could possibly count. They were in harmony with it, but far higher up the scale; cold, tingling, silvery voices. The second wonder was that the blackness overhead, all at once was blazing with stars. They didn't come out gently one by one, as they do on a summer evening. One moment there had been nothing but darkness; next moment a thousand, thousand points of light leaped out—single stars, constellations, and planets, brighter and bigger than any in our world . . . The earth was of many colors; they were fresh, hot and vivid. They made you feel excited until you saw the Singer himself, and then you forgot everything else.[10]

Can you picture it? The great lion singing creation into being? Echoing the reality of our own world that by His very breath, God brought forth life here too? Later in Narnia, after the land there has become barren and covered in snow, after the trees and the animals, the dwarfs and dryads have lost hope, many turned to stone by the evil of the White Witch, the *breath* of Aslan brings spring. It is his kiss that *awakens* those who are asleep, that melts the snow, that brings new life and fresh hope. Like Aslan, God is creating still, renewing us, softening us, drawing us to Him and bringing forth life in us with His song.

CHAPTER 3

To Leave Between

Our spiritual journey must lead through the desert or else our healing will be the product of our own will and wisdom. It is in the silence of the desert that we hear our dependence on noise. It is in the poverty of the desert that we see clearly our attachments to the trinkets and baubles we cling to for security and pleasure. The desert shatters the soul's arrogance and leaves body and soul crying out in thirst and hunger. In the desert we trust God or die.

DAN ALLENDER, *THE HEALING PATH*

The year I became ill, I still had strawberry shimmer smeared on my cheeks and watermelon gloss dotting my lips. I was mousy, with curly brown hair that crunched when I ran it through my fingers. I'd pour gel over all the tips and wrangle it through each strand just like the magazines showed. Looking in the mirror at my pink face, the artificial fruit scent wafting around me, I took in my reflection with awe. I felt so beautiful. I was innocent and walked with the confidence of Eden, of untainted innocence. I hadn't yet heard whispers that made me question who I was; no voices had contradicted my identity as a beloved daughter. In those days, looking out over the expanse of adolescence that lay before me was exciting.

Then, that winter, my cheeks were bright red—not with too-mature-for-me rouge, but aflame with fever. Strep throat choked and burned like fire, and no medicine was fast enough to chase the infection running through me. When the fever cooled a month later, an ember remained; I could feel a change. The remains of illness was still present. Before long it began to singe the strings that held me together. It felt like sharp sparks were flying underneath my skin, and I couldn't stop it.

The medical term is a mouthful: *Pediatric Auto-immune Neuropsychiatric Disorders Associated with Streptococcal Infections,* PANDAS for short, as if somehow the image of a fluffy bear might lessen the blow when you hear that your body will forever be a wilderness. Like rheumatic fever leaves traces of itself in the heart, PANDAS tears at the brain. It becomes its own master, always at war with your will, flaunting itself with uncontrollable movements. It's always clawing, cutting, on the prowl, gripping my body however it pleases. The look of it is awful: involuntary twitches and tugs that resemble hiccups and jerks. There is no peace. Every nerve is like a delicate tether, wound tight and bone dry. I've often wondered if I would just *snap*.

I don't remember making an intentional choice to hide myself away, but one day the girl filled with wonder, with the crunchy hair and watermelon lips, was just gone. I was overwhelmed by embarrassment and pain. I dreaded people and their questions, especially the ones I didn't know how to answer. I drew back, wanting to protect myself. I'd nod my head and try to act like I was okay, but every breath was measured, every step heavy. Every thought was focused on trying to control the fire and tame it before anyone could see it, before anyone knew. *Of course they all knew.* Middle schoolers are nothing if not incredibly adept at discerning differences among their peers. My friends saw the smoke. They saw the jerks in my arms and neck, twisting me, pricking me. They saw my eyes always diverting from their stares. They noticed that I said no to parties and laughter and anything resembling close friendship. I offered no explanation. I hid from school, taking handfuls of pills prescribed by doctors with sad eyes. I lay limp and curled on the couch for days at a time. The adults seemed more intent on keeping me comfortable, soaking in my sorrow, than in helping me fight. Looking back, this was my first brush with real, terrifying silence.

And I ran from it.

I kept running for years, putting on faces and putting on clothes I'd wallow beneath, ever the pretender. First I found a sort of freedom in being swallowed up by flannel, and the rhythm of grunge bands drowned out the panting of my racing heart. Later, I found a more acceptable peace in being the good girl, in roaming the world with an eye for adventure and then as a missionary, in soaking up travel and academics and then in making a home, and in my desire to live tidy and posed, perfect on the outside.

Decades later, when postpartum depression surfaced, I went on the run again. I harnessed my old instincts to hide when I felt desperate and harried. I packed the calendar to distract me from myself, from my pain. Busyness numbed me in a different way, my life so full on the outside that I never had to deal with what was lurking within. It was easy to hide behind a routine I could wholeheartedly throw myself into, easy to pretend to know the amity and reconciliation of God even as I felt a gaping hole in my heart. I desperately wanted to be still and pause and know He was close, but because I feared silence, I was afraid of the promise of *stillness*, and because I felt so alone, busyness became a friend.

Even as my heart cried out for peace, my body, I knew, would never, *could* never, be stilled. I would always be the girl who moved and felt like a marionette. My worth was driven by my performance while my nerves lay frayed and frail, a twitch or a jerk always ready to betray me. I would always (and still do) live fighting for a legato rhythm in life, soft and slow, in a body that screamed in jarring, staccato plinks and plunks. My need for stillness was spiritual—I was waking to this truth—but it was physical too. My very body was busy, as I was painfully aware every time I looked in a mirror or walked into a meeting. Could there truly be rest in my heart if my body wrestled with itself? Could I *be still* when the tension would never cease?

A Place to Pause

In music and poetry, a pause brings weight to what follows. In a sentence, a comma calls for a hesitation before a point is made, makes room for the thought to come. In music, a measure of rest builds our anticipation of the crescendo. And often, before the seasons of life that stretch and strengthen us, there are seasons of waiting, lulls of wondering and preparing for what lies ahead. They may appear empty and slow, meandering even, but the pause of these seasons ushers in the significance of the next measure of our lives.

I found myself forced into such a pause during that time as a new wife and mother. Our lives came to a full stop just as I was learning how to still my heart again. Our time in Germany was coming to an end, and Josh was ready to step forth into a new career. We weren't sure where it would take us, but we ended up in what seemed the most unlikely of places: our hometown.

There is a desert there, to the east of the little town of Cashmere, right in the center of Washington State. The division is clear, where the green and blue fade to clay brown. Going to college above Bellingham Bay meant lush green and blue and rainfall, and here, in our town, the days were dappled with sunshine year 'round, with snow dusting the evergreens in the wintertime. Ten minutes down the road lay the city of Wenatchee, cut straight through the center by the Columbia River, one side flourishing and fertile, the other dusty and bare. If you look way up on the plateaus and even into the base of the canyons, you will see acres of green. Orchards and fields of wheat thrive and blossom from the snowpack and all the sunshine flickering through. Irrigation lines carry water through ditches that weave from the river, nourishing areas that would otherwise lay dormant. Our home was tucked in there, among the pear trees and pines.

When you move somewhere new, the days are slow. Phone calls are scarce, invitations even more so because all your people, all your heartstrings, all the things you were supposed to do and places you were supposed to be have been left behind. Even with the warmest of welcomes, it takes a while to "break in" and make friends, or to get up the gumption to extend an invitation to someone yourself. The one grace in this is that your calendar is clear. You have a fresh start. For me, this meant my past dependence on noise and disharmony was exposed. As I was forced to slow, I began to find peace in the wilderness beyond my windows. All the twists and turns of my inner discord unraveled there beneath the wide expanse of sky and fresh air, floating among the aroma of blossoms and evergreens.

Affectionately, I refer to that season as our baby-making years. We added three more children to our family: Maia, spunky and fun, so full of belly laughs even as a baby; then our first boy, Jones, a carbon copy of his father, always whizzing around the girls; and at the tail end came Lael, delicate and doe-eyed, absolutely adored by all her siblings. Our little crew adventured together in the foothills, camped in the forest, learned how to share and how to love. Josh and I leaned into the rhythm of nighttime nursing and toddler meltdowns, of playdates and extended family dinners that stretched on past sunset. We took on the stable rhythm of our new tasks, mowing the grass up and down, line by line on Saturday afternoons, basking in the consistency of nap times and soccer games and church on Sundays. There was margin to dream and room to pray as quiet came easy in those steady days. It felt like God had tamed the storm swirling inside me by giving me an external slowness.

When I've thought about how we went home again, I've often considered the parable of the prodigal son. What happened to him after the feast, after he came home battered but welcomed with open arms? Did he settle back there with ease? Did he get married and have a few kids, work on his father's estate? Was he always at odds with his elder brother?

When we returned home, we were gathered into the arms of our parents and even our grandparents. I hadn't squandered a fortune like the prodigal son, but I had withdrawn from those who loved us, just as often as I'd run from the presence of God.

Still, they welcomed me. After years of feeling stretched thin, depressed, and unsure, I melted into their embrace.

We all need a way back. We need someone to hold the melody when our lives are out of tune. We need a friend or a grandmother ready to clasp our hand in her own and linger over our story. When we lift our heads and look toward home, we need to know there is someone on the road running toward us, eager to meet us. Somewhere between majesty and misery, heaven finds us in the barren wilderness of our deepest longings. This is where we can stop and embrace, where we can cease striving. When we've spent ourselves completely, we will be lifted into our Father's arms and met with tears of sheer joy and prayers of thanksgiving because of our return—because *He* has spent Himself completely *for us* too.

Finding the Name for What You Long For

I remember myself as a young girl, hammering my way through a piano piece I was attempting to master and first seeing the symbol for "rest" at the end of a bar or between chords. A sense of relief washed over me as I played. It meant I had a moment to find the keys I'd need to place my fingers on next. It gave me a beat of quiet to press the proper pedal before running up the next scale. The pause focused my fingers and footing and built up anticipation for resolution or excitement in the measures that would follow.

A rest is more than a hollow between notes; it is where the strings become steady and ready, waiting for the bow to stir them to life. When we slow and become subject to God's cadence, there is often a break before He brings the symphony—a measure, a bar, just a moment to exhale in expectation. Our valley years were this kind of rest: a stop we sensed would not last forever, but where my heart was learning to trust, where it was beginning to mend.

Silence was the landscape in which I found room to respond to God. As I continued my practice of praying the psalms and spoke my heart wholly into the void, I began to notice a word, one I'd seen since childhood but always skimmed right over. *Selah.*

If these pieces of Scripture were music, orchestrated prayers sung to a tune, *selah* was the signal to the musicians to rest, to pause, to cease. It was right there among the verses that held so much weight, that mirrored my own heart, my own longing. Even at the height of these measures, voices and instruments would hush. Silence would linger. There was space to take a breath. Release. Relief.

> But you, O Lord, are a shield about me,
> my glory, and the lifter of my head.
> I cried aloud to the Lord,
> and he answered me from his holy hill.
> *Selah*
> I lay down and slept;
> I woke again, for the Lord sustained me.
> I will not be afraid . . .
>
> PSALM 3:3–6[1]

> May the Lord answer you in the day of trouble!
> May the name of the God of Jacob protect you!
> May he send you help from the sanctuary

and give you support from Zion!
May he remember all your offerings
and regard with favor your burnt sacrifices!
Selah
May he grant you your heart's desire
and fulfill all your plans!

PSALM 20:1–4[2]

Let the enemy pursue my soul and overtake it,
and let him trample my life to the ground
and lay my glory in the dust.
Selah
Arise, O LORD, in your anger;
lift yourself up against the fury of my enemies:
awake for me; you have appointed a judgement.

PSALM 7:5–7[3]

There was a rhythm now to pouring out my heart: *Outcry. Rest. Relief. Praise.* My heart's howl, followed by grateful sighs. I was revived in this pattern, changed and re-oriented to praise and trust. When the tension still found in every muscle of my body threatened my new sense of calm, I could practice peace. Breathing in and out, I could whisper prayer, and instead of retreating, I could allow God to quiet my spirit as one swift jerk after another betrayed my will, contracting, seizing, and twitching to the involuntary rhythm of my illness. With these chronic staccatos, a body bound in busyness, stillness would always be a place of in-between.

Most scholars are in general agreement that *selah* is defined as a noun: a "pause, rest or interlude," but a few also translate it as a verb: "stop; listen" because what comes next is of particular importance. As I examined where these rests and pauses occurred—seventy-one times total in the book of Psalms—I began to see that *selah* in my own life, like *selah* in the psalms, often brought respite after I experienced exceptionally visceral and raw emotions, the very feelings I attempted to hide from God. And when these emotions were exhausted, they were met with rest; a proclamation of hope replacing a questioning cry.

This stillness and rest in the valley, wasn't this *selah* too? It was the in-between, like a beat in the Bible's poetry. I was living *selah*, beginning to see that in the moments I thought God was most silent, He was never absent. The stillness actually offered me more of Him. These moments were merely a rest in His larger composition. Praying the psalms had become my way of entering into music with Him. This kind of silence gives way to the sweetest tune we've ever known, a new chorus for our lives. But I couldn't have known then just how much I needed to learn my part.

CHAPTER 4

City Sojourners

Men did not love Rome because she was great.
She was great because they had loved her.

G.K. CHESTERTON, "THE FLAG OF THE WORLD"

While I was mothering in the valley, I was provided reliable days and a predictable schedule in which my soul began to mend. I settled into a pattern of reading and studying on my own, then giggling and making play dough with my children. I knelt down to their level, holding their chubby hands in my own as I listened and nurtured, surrendering my whole self, even my body, to this calling of caring for little ones. They were growing up right before me. *Nine, six, four, and two* . . . the numbers rolled off my tongue whenever anyone asked me their ages. But each time I recited it, I felt a bit shocked.

It had been nearly a decade of birthing babies and learning how to yield, to rise each morning with joy, to respond with affection to cries or fevers in the night, to slice PB&J into small triangles (because it was the preference of someone small), and to feign ecstatic surprise at the punch line of every knock-knock joke. Mothers live in the meter of steady days, ones of their own making. They are the center of the concentric circles that form a family, each person rising to greet the day and kissing it goodnight under their watch. They are the table setters, the drivers, the makers of celebrations and the initiators of memory. As the days pass, as time ticks by, a mother may not realize that she has become the metronome of her family.

For my heart, a slow learner, the steady days in our valley home were welcome. And then, we picked up that faithful rhythm and found ourselves in the fast-paced grid of New York City.

Like most sojourners to Manhattan, a job led us there. The Job. The dream work, the benefits package, the chance to make a splash in a company shaping its entire industry. Josh had been contracting with a company he loved, and they wanted him full time. But a full-time position meant living in New York City. We'd tiptoed around the idea of this move. We'd browsed real estate listings and looked at one another sideways when we watched movies set in the Big Apple. With our eyebrows raised, we'd turn to face each other on the couch and our looks would say, *Maybe I could . . . could you?* We casually brought up the idea to our families at Sunday brunch and then reeled it back in again when our mothers set down their forks and their eyes grew big. We awkwardly laughed in unison and shook our heads to reassure everyone. "Oh, what a silly idea. We never could, really. Don't worry, nothing to see here, no need to fret over the grandchildren." But we were itching to go.

In these situations, companies like to meet you, to size you up and sweeten the deal. They put candidates up in a hotel and take them to dinners at restaurants that serve itty bitty portions with artfully drizzled sauces, places where the low light makes everyone look like a movie star. Probably. At least, I imagined there was a lot of wining and dining and schmoozing when Josh flew across the country to spend a week in the Big Apple while I served corndogs from the microwave and only sometimes remembered to include a side of vegetables. But the moment he returned, I knew we were on our way. He looked boyish and fresh—excited. He was more than that; he was *inspired*. Of course we had to go.

My pulse rushed as our moving day approached. As I lined every box with tissue paper and packed it full, I would whisper vision to our four young babes, assuring them that it was exciting to set forth into something so grand.

From the window of the plane, the country had the appearance of patchwork. A new thread of our lives was being woven in among all the squares, tugged and tightened by the forward thrust of the jet engines. I couldn't have guessed there would be many times in the years that followed when I'd ponder that flight, how we'd become permanently hemmed into the geography of New York City.

My breath caught the moment we stepped outside the airport to hail a cab from Queens. In the west the air is wide, arid, clear, and passes right through you. But in the east, it prickles. It sits on your skin and twirls under your nose carrying the scent of hot dogs from the street cart, the stuffy smell of concrete, and the sweat of every passerby. New York almost instantly begins to stick. The opus and export of Manhattan is her culture, and the whole world is within her. In the span of only a few blocks, you can taste authentic gyro and kimchi, hand-cut linguine and dim sum. To live in New York is an education in the definition of hedge funds, the reality of corporate influence, and the necessity of social justice. On the sidewalks of one avenue, you'll pass boys lined up for their weekly fade at the barbershop, nannies pushing strollers for women wearing Italian leather flats, and Wall Street bankers buttoned up and wearing thin, silk ties. They all breathe the same thick air. New York is full of eight million people who couldn't be more different or more the same.

The Coreys were the first to knock on our door. Retired and in their seventies, they had moved into our building after a stint in Long Island to raise their children. Mrs. Corey and I would eventually come to exchange recipes and gather each other's mail. We brewed tea together in the afternoons, and Maia, who was in first grade that year, would snuggle up to practice reading aloud. *Dick and Jane* was her favorite in those early days of sounding out long and short vowels. *Can you see Dick? Do you see him? See Jane, see. See Dick run!* Mrs. Corey had learned to read from these stories too, so they shared a kinship right from the start. On rainy days, she would encourage me to let the children race or scooter down the length of our hallway to get out their wiggles. I wasn't sure of city etiquette, but she assured me it was just fine. So they'd shout and roar all the way past the double elevators to the opposite end of the hall.

That's how we met Nansy. Her two-year-old heard our troupe, and soon he was joining them in their evening escapades.

As the nights went by, more neighbors would arrive home and join us in their doorways, visiting and smiling at the ruckus we'd brought to the floor. Friendships wound between our tiny dwellings and up and down the stairwells. Someone was always there for dinners and dessert nights and to watch someone else's babies in a pinch. I had expected isolation in a city so big and so dense, but instead we found neighborhoods where people were truly known. The man at the bagel counter knew my children loved cream cheese “on the side,” and librarians tucked aside books by our favorite authors when we sauntered in. Our produce vendor would catch me walking by to let me know he had a new shipment of my favorite clementines, and workers at the cafes we frequented remembered us by name. We found fast friendship with other families, all transplants like us, and we latched on to one another to form our own safety net.

The older women in the neighborhood who had raised their own children in the ’50s and ’60s were permanent fixtures on the benches surrounding the playgrounds and fountains in the park. They taught me how to carry my purse safely on a city bus, how to read a subway map, and which neighborhood butcher was the best. They all seemed so vulnerable, but with every piece of advice they gave, I was reminded of their grit and their wits, and painfully aware that I was the one in a tender position, a stranger far from home. I tried to remember their words, tried to be prepared when I planned our days. I was determined to navigate this new cultural landscape, to make these women proud and cast off all my fears about how to fit in. But fear was there in the everyday unknown.

The first time I attempted to take the train by myself, I was sure I’d thought of everything. With my diaper bag looped over one shoulder, baby in the same arm, stroller folded and firmly gripped in the other, I wobbled to the underground. My three other children, all under the age of nine, were my little ducks in a row, neatly walking in front of me carrying scooters down the steps. In the August heat, the smell of garbage and urine from below caused my nose to crinkle. I drew in one deep breath from the outside and held it fast as we moved. “No! Sweetie! Don’t touch the wall!” I exhaled the last of the fresh, clean air as I pried my four-year-old away from a gray, moist goo dripping parallel to the railing. I nudged his tiny back with the sharp part of my elbow, the one still balancing the baby, while he moved closer, trying to examine the substance properly with his fingertips. I tried not to throw up when he wiped his nose with the back of his hand before I could reach the hand sanitizer. As the subway train approached, the shriek of its brakes and the click of the tracks echoed. The wind rushed from the tunnel where it emerged. *Ding*. The doors swung open and, holding hands together while still balancing the baby and bags and stroller, we made a leap on board toward the day's adventure. The doors closed, but my forgotten anxieties were opening right back up.

This juggling of children while hedging a myriad of potential dangers became my dance. I'd take a moment to tie up my sweaty hair, and I'd lose someone. I became adept at preparing perfectly for any time I spent outside the apartment or our safely gated playground. Stroller: check. First aid kit: check. Rain gear, water bottles, snacks, change of clothes: check-check-check. I was a catchall of security, outfitted to withstand all the elements of our new urban jungle. My world was expanding in vast proportions, but I was consumed with the small tasks that were my insurance. Just like those early days of motherhood, I clung to details as though our survival depended upon it. As our life swelled, my heart began to shrink.

It wasn't long before our apartment became a hideout on weekends. I could feel fatigue in my muscles, a tiredness that was layers deep. We brewed coffee and laid out Legos and puzzles, settled under blankets to watch movies in our pajamas, and ordered takeout for every meal, even breakfast.

We were still very much anchored in the everyday and the

mundane. For me, the excitement that accompanied passing by the Plaza Hotel or riding on a ferry in front of the Statue of Liberty was mellowed by the necessary school work and soccer practice and laundry. Days and hours in any family look much the same regardless of the background. Our struggle most of the time was finding room to manage tasks that were easy to accomplish in the suburbs but took much longer in our new context. I couldn't figure out how to organize all of us into 1,100 square feet, and Josh arrived home from work to a new arrangement of furniture on any given evening. Before I discovered grocery delivery services, I thought I might die carrying eight overfull bags home. Halle was in the fourth grade, but I loaded her with up with grocery bags and tons of responsibility to help me get through our days. She was a natural at logistics and could likely have managed us all on her own. Maia at six was cheerful and ready for adventure. She could help me keep four-year-old Jones close by or distracted with a fun game while I tried to buckle Lael, now an active toddler itching to join their fun, into her stroller. I'd learned my lesson about buckling Lael in fast when one of her attempts to escape had succeeded. She had hopped out to run alongside me, sending the stroller catapulting backwards to the ground, mixing all the milk and eggs together on the cement. Now I'd weigh down the back of the thing once she was secure and then loop more bags onto both my arms, all perfectly placed (until we hit a curb at the wrong angle). Even though we explored together every day, it took me months to learn which subway line to take, how to tell the difference between the express train and the local line, and even longer to know where we were when we emerged from underground.

But the children soon became experts on their scooters.

They learned how to stop at the corner of a building instead of the corner of the block in order to be safe in pedestrian traffic. They donned their little helmets and rushed out the door in their own mini-commuter style. Every once in a while, I'd look up from observing the little brigade screeching ahead and see the Empire State Building above us. I'd imagine all the screens and stories it had graced. Just like Deborah Kerr and Cary Grant in *An Affair to Remember*, we were all running in the direction of its spire, living this New York Childhood in its shadow.

Those moments of wistfulness re-inspired me to explore, and Saturdays became set apart for adventure. We'd trek to the museums, the Statue of Liberty, the Bronx Zoo, another section of Central Park. Captivated by the beauty and history, I'd catch myself stopping and pondering my surroundings while we waded through crowds. Nestled midway between the upper east and upper west sides is Turtle Pond, a sweet spot to feed the ducks, let the kids roam free, and serve up lunch from the waffle cart. Perched above it is Belvedere Castle. The first time we took a tour, I was struck by its bare stone interior—where were the bedrooms, the plush furnishings? Had it all been stripped away? The tour guide had to clue me in to the history: the castle had never been a private residence. It had been built for the people of New York as a conservatory and lookout. But it was so ornate, so beautiful. So thoughtful.

Someone in the past had considered us—considered me, in a sense. Considered that their investment in beauty would benefit future generations. The more I thought about it, the more I realized Belvedere Castle was just one example. Rockefeller Center, Central Park, and countless other landmarks shaping the skyline held the same character and purpose. Even Grand Central

Station, a place that could get by with simply being functional, has a delightful ceiling painted in the softest sea foam green with constellations glimmering in gold, and staircases curved in marble. Individuals in New York's past loved her. They built into her not just what was necessary but what was lasting, a loveliness that would permanently transform the landscape. When you are surrounded every day by that sort of legacy, it prompts you to question what, exactly, you are building. Did I ever really recognize that beauty imparted in our community could be lasting? Did I see a purpose to our mad dash days? As I pondered these things, I realized that my own vision was so very small, and really, an awful lot about *me.*

My whole heart for New York began to shift. What would happen if we lived aware of our resources and talents and personalities and intentionally poured them all into our new home? What if we raised our children to see the responsibility of bestowing loveliness? What if our affection for our city became so great that we sought the best for her?

One night, Halle found me staring out the kitchen window long after bedtime, at the end of a day when I'd snapped a few times and found myself racing through the city to get errands done. She was nearly ten, old enough to spot trouble. She'd been watching stress burn in me for weeks. She inched up beside me, and I stroked her hair.

"Mom, is this the real New York?"

"What do you mean, baby?"

"Well, it just feels like the same as home but in a smaller place where we can never have fun and we are always rushing. I thought New York would be full of lights and really exciting."

It was 9:30 on a Friday night. My response came as fast as I could think it.

"Get your shoes. We're going out."

Josh was sound asleep next to Lael's toddler bed; the only way her little body could relax was when he held her hand. I decided I'd leave a note. He probably wouldn't even wake up before I got back. I took no diaper bag, no stroller, no just-in-case-of-emergencies backpack. I only grabbed my wallet, and with a spirit of freedom, my girl and I slipped out the door.

"Mom, where are we going?!" Halle's eyes were wide and expectant; she could see the shift in me and knew a surprise was coming.

"You'll see," I said with a sly grin. As we hopped into a cab, I quietly directed, "43rd and 7th please." We'd shown the children this spot a few weeks before, but not at night. And in this case, it made all the difference. As we arrived in Times Square, Halle's grin turned into an awestruck giggle. We got out and walked, but we couldn't stop looking up, our senses straining to take in every flash and color. We caught the whirring of the Toys 'R' Us Ferris wheel, lit up and rising far above us and then plunging below street level, and with one look at each other, we knew it was our obvious destination; we had to experience it for ourselves. Up and around, again and again, we sat looking out over the city streets, full of so many different people, so much possibility. I felt my compressed heart expand just a little bit. Holding hands, we sat and stared at it all together and sighed with a satisfaction that we'd found a way to be here, in this city, at just this moment, and that somehow, we were making New York home. We knew, even as we tiptoed to our beds while the rest of the family slumbered, we would be forever changed by our own possibilities.

CHAPTER 5

A Curve in the Road

There, peeping among the cloud-wrack above a dark tor high up in the mountains, Sam saw a white star twinkle for a while. The beauty of it smote his heart, as he looked up out of the forsaken land, and hope returned to him. For like a shaft, clear and cold, the thought pierced him that in the end the Shadow was only a small and passing thing: there was light and high beauty forever beyond its reach.

J.R.R TOLKIEN, *THE RETURN OF THE KING*

I'd stopped driving once we arrived in Manhattan, but I often imagined what it was like to be a cab driver behind the wheel among so much honking and chaos. When I was a teenager, my Papa faithfully picked me up in his Jeep Wagoneer on Saturday afternoons, wearing his plaid shirt and brown slacks and his brown leather jacket. My parents were terrified to see me behind the wheel, so my grandfather had volunteered to teach me to drive. He began my education in the cemetery. With smooth straightaways and plenty of turns, it was the perfect place to learn. I could hit the gas in the smooth parts just right, but I always lost my confidence on the curves.

"Darlin' you don't have anything to worry about. Everyone here is already dead."

He said this every week. He waited for just the right moment to deliver the line, and then he'd chuckle and grin, and my resolve would return while we laughed together. I'd try again. Inevitably I'd jerk the old Wagoneer and throw my foot too hard and then slam the brake, sending us backward to collide with the headrests.

These were our Saturdays, until one afternoon right near a turn that always sparked my anxiety, he had me pull over. The fresh air felt good, and we walked for a moment before I realized that he wanted to show me his plot, the place where one day he would be laid to rest. *No, no, no.* I wasn't ready to think about it. He was so young and vibrant for a grandfather. He would live forever, I thought. He would be with me for so many moments that mattered throughout my life. We had many more years to go boating and water skiing, to read the newspaper and listen to Andy Williams together, to make sure the family cabin was stocked with Honey Bunches of Oats. We'd dance at my wedding, and he'd welcome my children at their births, anxious and pacing in the lobby of the hospital as I labored with each one.

When heaven began to pull Papa home, I was no longer a teenager naïve to grief. I was a mother of four, a grown-up with a mortgage. By then, Parkinson's had been weakening his frame for a decade. I snuggled up close and held my grandfather's hand

and all my worries about how to say goodbye came rushing back, as heavy as they had been during that driving lesson years before. Lael, my baby at the time, tiny and angelic, slept on my lap in a purple cotton dress when I leaned in and said goodbye to Papa. As she was breathing in new life, he slowly exhaled his.

I didn't see it yet, but this exchange would become a familiar one. Breathing in, breathing out. New life and letting go, cycles of welcomes and goodbyes to mark my days.

Grieving as the World Rejoices

My doctor told us the news on a Friday. Our baby's heart had stopped beating. It was during our second year in New York, and I'd been out shopping for stocking stuffers all afternoon. The holiday markets filled all the parks with peppermint-striped tents, and the street vendors were selling brown bags of roasted chestnuts on every corner. The ice rinks were open, and we had tickets to see the Rockettes perform at Radio City Music Hall. I'd spent so much time daydreaming in front of shop windows, taking in their meticulous designs, that I had to hail a taxi to make it to my appointment on time. It was sure to be quick. I was in the second trimester of my pregnancy, and the visit was supposed to be routine, only a simple check-up. Then came the blow.

She gave us the weekend to decide what to do—let labor come on its own or have surgery. It was Christmas, and I was numb, forced to choose how to let a child fall from my womb as the whole earth rejoiced in the miracle of birth. But her life poured out on Christmas Day. We trimmed the tree and tucked gifts beneath it the same night I began to miscarry, and I wondered if I'd ever enter into Advent with expectant joy again. All my hope had been exchanged for grief, every twinkle and glimmer of light was a reminder of life snuffed out. After a long labor and contractions, I birthed her, still and tiny. We cupped her body in our hands as Josh and I wept at a promise that was unfulfilled—held forever, but hollow.

The Silent Night, so beautiful to many, became our terror.

We buried her in the cemetery in our valley, right near that curve of road that made me jerk and then brake, where I'd had so many stops and starts. She's buried there, in the place where I began to realize that death jerks us around too, that grief comes fast and goes slow. She's buried right next to my grandfather. We named her Thea Nöel. Thea comes from a name that means gift. Because God gives, even in death. Even at Christmas.

Miscarriage is one of those words that causes people's faces to crease with compassion. Their eyes reflect questions as they wonder what to say, how long they should linger with you in sadness, which moment is appropriate to shift gears and change subjects. It's odd to tell your friends that you are grieving something that, to them, was invisible. I found myself longing to release them from the awkwardness of not knowing how to respond while simultaneously clinging to them in desperation. I needed them.

The Hurricane that Sent Me Spinning

A year later, a storm blew through the East Coast, and the waters began to rise. From ten stories up, we watched the waves roll in with the tide. Every minute they inched closer, hugging the red brick of our building and then splashing out again to the grass where we'd just had a picnic lunch earlier in the day. Lapping back and forth, the tide moved deeper into lower Manhattan, filling the streets until we sat, stuck in our building as eight feet of water from the East River pooled in our lobby.

Hurricane Irene had come to visit us the previous summer, and I'd loaded up on batteries, an emergency radio, and cases of bottled water. We were ready for our first East Coast hurricane. And then, before she reached the north, Irene hedged right and emptied across the Atlantic. I suppose that's why when we heard about Hurricane Sandy, we shrugged and assumed she would be much the same. But as we watched the waters rise inside the designated safe zone, witnessed abandoned cars floating into view, and heard great trees crack, we knew this storm was one we could not weather alone.

When the East River Estuary receded, a salty musk loomed. Darkness and chill hung in the air and in our windowless hallways. The lines for hurricane evacuations in New York City have been redrawn because of what happened in our neighborhood that night, because we'd been told to sit tight and we'd be safe, but then were trapped. To get out, we needed to march down ten flights of stairs to the emergency exit, as our elevators had been flooded and wouldn't function without electricity. The lobby doors had been blown open wide by the raging wind, and in their absence an officer from the NYPD was standing guard around the clock, our own sentinel. We all emerged slowly, finding safety in meeting one another in familiar corners. For two days, we ferried medicine and food to neighbors too weak to attempt the stairwell. Our local markets were candlelit and cash only, and almost everyone was making a run for food that wouldn't spoil. Friends reunited on short walks as we inspected the damage, the men unshaven, the women wearing two-day-old topknots, and all of us a little worse for wear. To our children it was all a game: cooking over the camping stove, layering on warm down jackets, and playing board games by candlelight. They were like grand adventurers, up and down the stairs every time the dog whined and needed to trudge out. They greeted the police officer with a high five, and by the second day they were racing to be the first to answer the knock of Red Cross volunteers delivering sandwiches and comfort. We peeled off the waxed paper and swallowed them quickly at the table that just one week earlier had been full of classmates completing science experiments, plates of teetering blueberry and banana muffins, and hot coffee.

Eventually the city buses decided not to venture below 23rd Street. The darkness downtown was too risky, so the last stop left strangers organizing in pairs to find their way together by flashlight. Many walked more than a few miles until they were safely home.

That was the same night our men rallied for our elderly neighbor, Fred, on the twelfth floor. He was ill and in desperate need of dialysis, so they teamed up to carry him down the stairs on a gurney, calming him in the darkness with steady words and strong limbs. I squeezed his wife's hand as the men, thrown together by the crisis, lowered him down.

I couldn't help being reminded of the friends who'd banded together to deliver one who was weak to the feet of Jesus. Do you remember them? In Luke 5, Jesus was teaching to a large crowd. People crowding in had come from every village in Galilee and from Judea and even Jerusalem. Luke tells us that as Jesus was healing the sick, some men tried to carry their paralyzed friend to Jesus, but they couldn't get through the throng. They had likely already transported him some distance, they were probably tired and ready to set him down, but they had to keep circling. Jesus was inside a house, and these men decided to climb to the roof, remove the thatch and lower their friend through the ceiling! Can you imagine them, maneuvering him on a mat, probably something like a stretcher, up to the roof? When this man was unable to bring his own body to the feet of the great healer, his friends did everything they could to bless him and lift him up. And once this paralyzed man was face to face with Jesus, he was restored. He even carried his own mat out of there.

In our post-Hurricane Sandy days, this was the only metaphor I could find to express why we felt so safe and so content; so many friends were carrying our mat, lifting us toward healing when we were weak and overwhelmed. Their care equipped us to carry the mats of others in turn.

We had no clue what was going on outside our own chaos, but the rest of the world was watching New York too. Members of the American Legion knocked on the door of our relatives in our little valley so far across the country—men in their eighties, veterans, and community servants who were eager to help anyone affected by the winds and waves of Hurricane Sandy. They delivered a large check to my mother-in-law with faces long and expectant. We were able to buy supplies, food, and more medicine for our elderly neighbors and even spend a night in a hotel to bathe and sleep where it was warm.

When the lights flickered back on and heat raced up through the pipes, my heart warmed to see our building come back to life. Surely this was what *home* felt like, this community that offered kindness in the storm.

But we had only just begun to get acquainted with the darkness. By December I couldn't breathe. My little boy couldn't either. Jones was six now, and night after night his small chest would heave and tighten as the air grew thin. We gasped through asthma treatments and stood in the steam of the shower in the middle of the night. Sometimes we rode the big elevator to the lobby and rushed out the door to wash our lungs with cold air. There was that looming musk, salty, sticky, hanging heavy since the hurricane. It turned out black mold was burgeoning in the basement eleven floors below, where so much of the East River had flooded in. Through the steam pipes it crept up, mushrooming into our apartment and silently poisoning our air. We had to leave. We couldn't stay. Our fragile sense of home felt violated. The hope we'd felt in our newfound community was just a vapor.

Maybe from the stress, maybe from the mold, or maybe for no reason at all, another heartbeat registered flat that next Christmas. Another baby, gone. I couldn't move. I felt like I was living in a horrible recurring dream. Another miscarriage. Another year to play the part of perky mom while I screamed on the inside and raged with grief. Death seemed to be a creeping blackness that I could not escape. Overtaking my heart, overtaking my home, lurking mutely, on the prowl for its pound of flesh.

There were too many curves in the road. And my instinct was to jerk, to hide away and retreat as they approached. For me, to stay in New York City had become a risky bend in the road, and I sensed myself ready to run again. My impoverished body and heart craved relief. I wanted to run again, to a controlled circumstance where I could feel safe. I'd been distracting myself from my grief by pining for a new experience with no mistakes in it, no storms, no death, no creeping mold. I began to picture raising my children in the country again, driving a car, buying toilet paper in bulk with room to store it.

I would often succumb to my urge to wander around Pottery Barn, where I'd fold my body into the couch cushions, waltz through the tile bathrooms, and imagine our own monogrammed towels and a bowl of variegated loofahs. I wanted to have it all, to consume it all, to fill my hollow with every pretty little thing I could find. Just as I'd tried to fill my fear of silence with busyness, I wanted to fill my ache of empty with *stuff.* But every time I went out shopping, I came home with a bit of resentment in the bottom of my bag. I kept imagining a home where my children didn't have to squeeze into bunks and day beds at night, where they'd have space to roam free. Every nerve felt exposed, every impulse misplaced in the temporal instead of the everlasting. I wanted nothing more than to escape and move on to the next place, the next thing.

One evening, I peered out a cab window on my way home and looking up, caught the reflection of the night on the skyscrapers whizzing past, the fragmented light bouncing off buildings and bridges and street lamps. But never the moon, I noticed, never the stars. The city had swallowed them up whole and reflected only itself. My own heart caught light only in fragments these days too, shards blurred and quick, too fast for me to truly see. With every bone-tired breath, we'd been determined to stay in New York City. But could we? *Should* we? Was any dream job worth this much? Our coffers were nearly empty, our emotions all but spent. How could we keep up with the demands and the cost of living in a city that promised so much but never seemed to be done taking from us? From my very womb?

As these thoughts raced through my mind, I looked back inside the cab toward Josh and spoke my fears aloud.

"I just don't know if we can do this anymore. If we keep

going like this, I'm afraid we'll have nothing left. I'm so frazzled and threadbare. It's just not sustainable."

It wasn't the first time I'd said these words. They were on repeat, one of a bevy of phrases I often used to put words to my fears, to plop them in Josh's lap when I was feeling particularly anxious. When he finally spoke, his words resonated deeply with me.

"Maybe our life is more about how we invest than what we store."

I knew my circumstances were clouding my resolve. But maybe I didn't need an escape; maybe I needed *selah*. I began to ask God to give us a pause to reorient our hearts to where He had called us.

It came in the most unexpected way: the black mold became a blessing, a catalyst in a search for a new apartment. The process can take months, but we had to outrun the bad air that wrung our lungs. The beauty of working in the tech industry as Josh does is the flexibility to work remotely from time to time, so while we continued our search for a new place to call home, we decided to fly west to visit family for an extended stay so that we could elude storms, steam pipes, and death. We were returning to the place where we'd encountered the rest that had transformed our hearts, where even the winter chill would be welcome. I felt buoyed by the thought of days full of races on sleds and hot cocoa afterwards, blanched foothills and towering evergreens, reading stories under knitted blankets by a toasty fire.

We arranged to have all our belongings put into storage while we went away, and I knew as we packed up to depart that I would never enter my first New York apartment again. I would never walk through the door to find Mrs. Corey at our table with a cup of tea or hear the children rumbling through the common hallway after dinner. A car service slid up to the curb to carry us to the airport. Josh hustled the children and bags downstairs, but I felt a pull, a knot in my stomach that caused me to linger. I stood facing the living room, speechless and disappointed, and then yelled into the emptiness, "Well, goodbye then!" I slammed the door hard with a huff. I was saying goodbye to all those sweet possibilities I'd imagined on the Ferris wheel that night with Halle. To the dashed hopes of nestling two more children to my breast, holding them in my arms. I was casting it all off as I slammed the door. But grief has a way of sticking, like the humid city air on our skin, like the mold in our lungs.

A Winter Respite

There are only a few ways to enter our familiar little valley. We usually take the pass. That's what the locals call the road that winds between the Cascade Mountains, bridging the urban culture of Seattle and the quiet orchards and farms of eastern Washington. Evergreens line the way, and peaks rise and fall in the foreground as the pavement bends round and then back again, climbing steadily with every turn. I can't count the number of times I've driven this road, on these two lanes stretched to connect east and west, suspended above the rest of the world. When it snows, the sky is swathed in pink and grey. Moonlight diffuses on the sides of the hills, and the way the clouds hover makes them glow just before they let their flakes loose to dance. As we followed the curves toward our town below, snow transformed the trees, made its bed over the dirt and the dust. As it fell, everything in our view was cloaked in white.

This is where, as a child, I first came to know the secret stars—the ones hidden in the haze of any city or town, the ones you have to climb high to glimpse. When I was small, my parents used to set up our bright red telescope in the backyard after dark. They'd pull my little sister and me from the warmth of our beds and wrap blankets around us, and we'd go outside beneath the open sky to take in the sparkling light, shining even more clearly in small clusters through the telescope lens. We were a family that attended Sunday school every week, and my parents spoke daily of Christ's love for us, but it was these nights under the stars that captured my imagination about God.

For about a decade I was so taken with the sky that I wanted to be an astronaut. I even went to space camp in fourth grade because I dreamed of soaring through the universe.

Scientists tell us now that they can hear radio waves in space. Really hear them. I've listened to the recordings. When I took my children to the planetarium, we shushed one another to catch the echo pinging back to earth between the chains of satellites. It's a bit like the fuzz you hear on old televisions when the screen goes all gray and black. It's muffled but it's there. Sound, the planetarium exhibit explains, precedes the expansion of the stars. Before the universe moves out and onward, before creation expands, there is a noise—or rather, I believe, a voice. Audible. Present. And now, *heard*.

> By the word of the Lord the heavens were made, their starry host by the breath of his mouth.[1]

The universe unceasing. The voice of God that is never silent, but always with us. He commands the stars to sing and to dance even now, with a tenor so powerful it registers on human technology.

We were purposing to listen, to lie fallow in the desert, under the stars. I began to imagine again the God who held all things together. Who was holding *me* together. Whose voice and breath created the vast wonder outside my window. Like the psalmists meditating on the wonder of God, his awe and majesty drawing them closer to him, the whisper of winter wind drew me to his voice too.

I signed the kids up for ski lessons and steeped myself in books and tea at the lodge. I didn't want to leave the soft caramel and white of those hills or the billows of my own down comforter each morning. My body and my heart needed time to heal. I was becoming gradually more aware each day that there was a desert place that existed in my own heart and not just in my geography.

I thought of the stars again, their silver light on snow, twirling, commanded to move ever forward by a voice advancing creation still. The melody of the stars was the Word, that never silent voice, tucked into my own heart. It was healing and wholeness and beauty itself, and as I walked those few months in the mountains, it was constantly ringing in my ears, reviving me, readying me. Drawing me close to the Creator of it all so that I could be sent back into the thick of a busy place, and keep a calm poise of heart. I had a sense that's what finding *selah* was really about: a calm not in the place of the storm, but in the midst of it.

CHAPTER 6

The Color of Peace

Ah, that miracle! Ah, that sweet miracle! It was not men's grief, but their joy Christ visited. He worked his first miracle to help men's gladness."

FYODOR DOSTOYEVSKY, *THE BROTHERS KARAMAZOV*

Bang! Bang! Bang!

The muffled sound followed me down the hall from under the floorboards and slowly grew louder, angrier. The pounding was coming from the apartment below. Off and on for days, our new neighbors had been beating on their ceiling to tell us to be quiet. When the moving trucks had pulled up to our new building on Manhattan's Upper West Side, we unpacked with vigor. The search had taken months, but we had finally found a new home. We had left the haven of our old apartment building. Left the Coreys and afternoon tea, left our band of hurricane survivors, and landed in the only apartment we could find after FEMA relief funds had flooded the real estate market. Our apartment was half the size of our first, but it had one glory: it was right next to Central Park, which would become our new backyard. Grass and ponds, trees and trails all captivated, rivaling our earlier dreams of city living.

We had not however, expected this pounding.

We'd taken to walking on padded feet and bought foam liners to go underneath all the rugs, but nothing seemed to appease the apartment dwellers below us. As my kids stopped giggling to listen to the noise too, I whispered with relief, "Oh, it finally stopped!" and made a move toward the kitchen to pull noodles out of the pantry for dinner.

Nope.

There it was again. *Bang! Bang! Bang!* Josh came out of the bedroom and stared at me.

"I don't even know! Don't ask me about it!" I said sharply, exasperated, jaw clenched, slicing mushrooms and willing the pasta to cook already so I could sprinkle mozzarella over the top, serve my babies at the table, and move on to homework and bedtime. The constant thumping was my tipping point. With every *thwap* that reverberated beneath us, my pulse increased, faster, louder, tugging at my patience as the kids played in the next room and laughed at every punchline of their TV show on cue.

Bang! Bang! Bang!

"Babe, I think it's their broom!"

Josh seemed genuinely interested, entertained even. The thumping had been going on all day and all the day before, and I wasn't quite as intrigued.

"Do you think they are actually standing on their furniture with their broom to hit the ceiling? They must be really mad at us."

They were. I know because they soon told us. They chose to confront us the next week at my daughter's birthday party. As ten little girls snuggled up with popcorn and licorice for a movie night, I began to light candles on the cake. The children were all murmurs and excitement and smiles. The thudding had been going on then too. Even though I'd left a note in their mailbox letting them know we'd have guests. I'd purposefully made sure all the girls would be gone by eight, still early for a Friday night. But then a knock at my front door was delivered with such force that all the pictures in the entryway fell off the wall. We could hear her yelling outside the door, accusing and angry, and as Josh slipped outside to talk to her away from the children, my neighbor thrust the door wide open and stepped inside to howl right at their sweet faces.

"WHAT are you doing up here!? WHAT is this racket? WHO are all these children?! THIS IS WAR!"

Those were her last words before retreating. She declared war on me. For walking in my own apartment. Sometimes for dropping the peanut butter jar while I was making lunch. Always for laughing. Always for closing the door to the bathroom. My daily life was offensive to the woman who lived below me, and her threats were hurled at us daily via the end of her broom with a *Bang! Bang! Bang!* When we came face-to-face, she huffed at my babies, she told me she would have us evicted. I smiled or made a beeline away from her and whispered to the kids to just stay calm. When her husband yelled through the vents that he was going to come and chop our heads off, and again, when he screamed that he had a gun and wasn't afraid to use it, we called the police. I stood shaking as the NYPD huddled in our kitchen, their radios humming with dispatch communications and beeps the whole time. They took a statement, they taught us how to document every incident, they walked us through how to build a case. They used words like *harassment* and *protective order*, and my mind spun. I didn't feel safe at home.

A New Perspective Brings Rest

It had been nearly a year since our few months in our valley, since our season of rest and recovery. We had been revived, steadied, eager to return home, but the weight of the past year and diving back into city life had never fully lifted. We were sustained by our rest, but ever aware that it was draining from us by the day. On top of the harassment and the tight space, our whole family came down with mono. You know, the illness that makes you drift off to sleep in the middle of the day, that leaves you lagging, unable to take another step. We were stumbling through our days, trying to stay awake until dinner, trying to laugh about the stress of it all with friends, when we were faced with the stuff of urban legends: bedbugs.

I found one bug. That's it. The inspectors sent it to a lab. It was confirmed, and then the decontamination was underway. When I attended my first mothers' group years before, one woman had confided that she prayed against an infestation of bedbugs every day. Heads nodded around the room as everyone else admitted that they too waged spiritual battle against these creatures. Not me. I had neglected this entire area of my prayer life and now here we were: easy targets. We were quarantined, cut off from community, telling only the closest friends in faint whispers not to worry about what had become of us. We'd see them in a month or so. *Please don't tell anyone. Say we have the flu.*

If you are ever the victim of such a horror yourself, what follows is my contribution to the best practices and procedure for ridding bedbugs from your dwelling:

1. Call your building super. Listen to him gasp. Wait thirty minutes until he has alerted a professional to come and inspect your apartment. Don't get excited about this fast, efficient level of service; they are only attentive because they live in fear of this infestation spreading. They are only here because they don't want your sad state of affairs to blackball them on every real estate site in Manhattan and scare potential renters (AKA money) away.
2. Be prepared for everyone in your building to glare at you and know that your apartment is the epicenter of their worst city-living fears. You have brought this plight upon them all. Every unit on your floor and on the floors above and below yours must also be inspected for bedbugs. This is how you've been found out by all your neighbors. It is the health code. It's the law that their mattresses must be overturned by inspectors, stat. It is inevitable that they will be filled with anxiety at the prospect of also being victims of bedbugs.
3. Within twenty-four hours, you must bag up every soft thing you own. This includes clothes, sheets, pillows, toys, stuffed animals, draperies, towels, shoes, cloth napkins and every last tiny doll outfit that you were crazy enough to buy for your daughters last Christmas. Everything. ALL OF IT. You must call around to various laundromats to inquire about their decontamination services, because this is a chore you cannot complete yourself. You would contaminate the public laundry of your building and it would take seventy billion years to finish (give or take a few) because remember, you are washing All. The. Things. You will happily pay

outrageous amounts of money to have everything you own washed in special formula and removed from your home by gloved men with wide eyes. They will not even tell their wives about this.

4. Prepare for fumigation. After all soft items are removed from your apartment, you too must be removed. Find somewhere to stay for 24–48 hours, but DO NOT convey under any circumstances that you are looking for shelter due to fumigation of bedbugs. Your battle must remain a secret, or you and all your babies will most likely be sleeping on the sidewalk.
5. When you return to your apartment, the strictest protocol must be followed. Continue to keep all soft possessions in sealed bags. Only pull out what you absolutely require. Consider using a hairdryer instead of towel-drying after a shower and having children only wear swimsuits. Get used to the sound of crying and the sight of tears when they are not able to play with all their things currently enclosed safely in said bags. When you leave the apartment, you must: (1) strip out of any clothes that have been worn in the apartment, (2) place contaminated clothing in a sealed bag so as not to spread the hazard outside of your apartment, (3) put on fresh clothes, (4) try to dress as near to the front door as possible so that you may exit quickly and not incur the possibility of contaminating the "safe" clothes. You must repeat this ritual every time you leave your home. You must double wash all clothing from the contamination bag before placing it in a sealed "safe" bag and taking it back to the apartment. Continue this regimen for two weeks.

6. Under no circumstances mention bedbugs on public transportation. Panic may ensue.
7. Place all bedding and any contaminated linens in sealed bags. Leave apartment once again for 24–48 hours while second round of fumigation occurs.
8. Repeat step 4 for two more weeks until third round of fumigation occurs.
9. Fast and pray that the inspector does not find any other evidence of bedbugs.
10. Cautiously unpack your belongings, consider anointing every doorpost with holy oil, and begin nightly prayer vigils against bedbugs, which you now know you should have been doing since moving to Manhattan in the first place.

At some point during this timeline, I think between steps 7 and 8, Josh's parents were scheduled for a visit. When they arrived, my mother-in-law looked into my eyes and pulled out her cell phone. She went to work making plans to help me survive. The first step was to shoo me out the door to take a walk and get a deep breath.

I let the stress of the neighbors' harassment and the bedbug infestation roll off my shoulders as I walked straight across Central Park to see an old friend: the Metropolitan Museum of Art. I made my way up the giant staircase and veered left. The soles of my shoes echoed in the great hall; even among a crowd, the mood is always hushed. I floated through the tourists, beyond statues from the Greek and Roman periods to a column from the Temple of Artemis, one of the seven wonders of the world. Beyond it lay the elevators that would carry me to the second-floor galleries. Degas, Van Gogh, Monet, Cezanne—they were all there, hanging under soft light in bold strokes and foggy pastels, stretched across the walls. After all the grey of my current predicaments, I practically thirsted for their colors. I passed by violets and waterlilies, but it was the waves that transfixed me.

Perched on a plush velvet bench, I stared at Monet's *Regatta at Sainte-Adresse* in the corner of a gallery wall lined with sailboats and shorelines. I tried to imagine a time when I'd seen a man sit on the sand in a three-piece suit to take in a race at the seaside and wondered what it must have been like to be a lady then, layered in crinoline and petticoats. Clouds spread across an indigo sky, and the blue and green raced in spiral brushstrokes through the canvas. *Regatta* is serene, a painting that illuminates an innocent point in history. It captures the scene wholly, and I realized I'd become lost for a moment in the 1860s. A school group entered, and I smiled at little girls uniformed in navy rompers, yellow buttons done up at their shoulders, their white collars all crinkled and matted in varying directions. They moved through the room single file, with tired eyes and bored sighs, as their teacher waxed poetic about Impressionism. From the sight of them, they'd been at it for a while. Two of them wiggled in near me on the velvet bench to tie their shoelaces, deep in concentration as they held the strings: *under, over, around the tree goes the rabbit and into the hole*. I took my cue and scooted, then stood to give them a wide berth for their work.

I looked back at the painting of the waves and the bleached sails, as if to whisper, *It'll just be a minute. I'll be right back*. But from there, the entire regatta had shifted. The line of the shore and the sky had found a new symmetry. The water seemed truly fluid, moving. I would have missed it if I'd kept looking only head-on, if my reverie had not been interrupted. The regatta was, of course, very much the same as it has been since Monet's brush first dipped into turquoise paint. *I* had changed. My vantage point had shifted, altering what I saw.

As I reentered my apartment later that afternoon, I kissed my drowsy boy's forehead, already thinking through the next steps in our war against bedbugs. But the perspective of the regatta at a slant was still fresh. I considered my invigorating interlude at the Met earlier, in light of the events of our past year.

The circumstances we faced upon our return to Manhattan were not improved; looking at it only head-on, anyone might say they were probably worse. But with each blow to our calm, my heart remained, somehow, steady. I believe it's because the previous winter had offered me valuable perspective. I had breathed long and deep in the valley, had been bolstered by rest, by the waves and the stars and the voice of God. There was a peace carried within me. I had been reoriented in the valley—in the space where stillness speaks and changes us so that we can press forward.

I began to realize how the breath of *selah* didn't just revive me, but changed me wholly. In the psalms, as the pattern of prayer travels from pain to praise and back again, God Himself is there, changing the perspective of the heart. He had been restoring me, letting me stretch out before He did something new. And now, even in the tumultuous circumstances of our illness and our bedbugs and our bitter neighbors, He was filling me up with Himself. It was just a slight shift, a turning of the spirit, but it changed the way I saw everything and colored my world with peace.

The First Miracle

When Jesus made His public debut, it was at the request of His mother. She nudged Jesus at a wedding feast to let Him know they had run out of wine. He asked her, "What does this have to do with me?" but instead of responding to Him, she told the servants, "Do whatever he tells you." His mother must have known His heart for people, His heart for the happiness of this new couple. Jesus told the servants to fill the jars full of water and deliver them to the host. And when the host drank, he discovered the water had turned to wine. The first miracle was to aid in merriment. Christ's public introduction was to say, I want more for your delight, more for your felicity. I will take the water of your life and make it wine.

The miracle in *me* was in meeting the reveler of beauty, of joy, right in the middle of my chaos. It was finding Him in an interlude that began to turn out peace because He was there. God was teaching me that rest matters as much as the words or cries surrounding it. That there was significance in experiencing an interlude of beauty, like I had standing before the waves of the Monet at the Met, like I had in the valley, and in the mountains under a blanket of stars. Respites of beauty and delight shape us, remake us even, and fuel all the work of our lives that will come. Jesus was making wine, bringing delight, forging rest, and giving me fortitude as I walked with Him. A small word can change everything, and in the space of a few notes, in a *selah*, I was finding how to come face to face with the God who has spoken to create and is speaking still.

CHAPTER 7

How His Music Heals

"You mean you're comparing our lives to a sonnet? A strict form but freedom within it?"
"Yes. . . . You're given the form, but you have to write the sonnet yourself. What you say is completely up to you."

MADELINE L'ENGLE, *A SWIFTLY TILTING PLANET*

"Goodnight my love . . . and may your dreams be, sweet my love . . . and tomorrow, be sunny and bright . . . and bring . . . you closer . . . to Jesus."

I remember the night we sang those words as new parents. The stars were sparkling for us again as we drove with the sunroof open to the night and rounded the slight road that skimmed alongside the lake. It was late, too late to be driving home with a toddler fighting sleep after a night spent eating and chatting in the cool of the summer with friends. Josh started to sing first, and then I chimed into the Hawaiian lullaby we used to shush

Halle to sleep most nights. Usually we had an audience of plush toys as we rocked her in the chair handed down by her grandmother. Before long, the familiarity of the tune and the lyrics we whispered together from the front seat calmed her tiny body, and she released a series of sighs and little sniffles as her eyelids grew heavy and she fell fast asleep. That little made-up song has been the lullaby of all my babies since. It's on rotation with James Taylor's "Lonesome Road," and "Tomorrowland." Each of our children knows the tune and the key. Each one has been found singing it to comfort another sibling or a baby doll "resisting nap time." Music does soothe, doesn't it? It calms us and connects us in ways science is only just beginning to understand.

We are learning now that music also heals. In neonatal intensive care units, where the very smallest preemies receive care, the rule for decades has been to decrease all stimulation, to mimic the womb as much as possible as they develop, but in recent years it has become common practice to also offer music therapy. When a guitar or cello is played, when songs are sung, parents and medical teams tell us that the faces of these little babies actually change. They almost instantly become calmer and less fidgety, and often their eyes will open. Their vital signs change too. As music plays, their oxygen levels go up and their heart rates stabilize. It's not just preemies either; babies who are experiencing withdrawals from drug abuse in the womb and those suffering from birth defects are shown to have a decrease in pain as a result of music therapy. Christy Merell, a music therapist at St. Louis Children's Hospital, says that many of her former patients have been known years later to sing the songs that were played for them, even without any tangible memory of their weeks or months in the NICU.[1] The way music is soaked into their lives is very much like the way we all learn language, and these babies are learning language *through* music. Merell continues, "Music has a cool way of working around frayed ends in the brain and either re-building old pathways or creating new ones."[2] Is it any wonder, then, that as parents we naturally sing to soothe our children? We sing lullabies to calm, to comfort, and to connect. We are all wired to respond to, resonate with, and even come alive through song.

It's no surprise, then, that those passages of Scripture that teach us how to feel and lament and express also give the church a heritage of music. Not only the poetry and prayer book of the Bible, the book of Psalms is our *songbook*. We first see King David, who is mentioned in Chronicles, as the sweetest psalmist in Israel, organizing orders of musicians in the tent pitched for the Ark of the Covenant. Can you picture it? The harps and lyres, the cymbals, all joining together with voices in the wilderness of Israel? Worship and lament and praise rising under the sky, dancing through the sunlight and traveling on the wind, slipping through the curtains of the tent, carried before the presence of God there in the Ark? What holy ground must have stirred in the dust beneath the sandals of God's people as they assembled there to be near Him.

In the second temple, psalms were sung in a special pattern depending on whether they were used in daily services or reserved for holy days and particular seasons of the year. This pattern is still used today in the Hallel, the template and guide for Jewish ceremonies and festivals. In the book of Matthew, we even see Jesus singing hymns with His disciples on the night He would be betrayed. Because it was the Passover, it is likely that He was singing from the Hallel, as that would have been the custom of His time. Passover tradition most likely included the singing of the last great Hallel, Psalm 136:

> Give thanks to the Lord, for he is good.
> *His love endures forever.*
> Give thanks to the God of gods.
> *His love endures forever.*
> Give thanks to the Lord of lords:
> *His love endures forever.*
> to him who alone does great wonders,
> *His love endures forever.*
> who by his understanding made the heavens,
> *His love endures forever.*
> who spread out the earth upon the waters,
> *His love endures forever.*
> who made the great lights—
> *His love endures forever.*
> the sun to govern the day,
> *His love endures forever.*
> the moon and stars to govern the night;
> *His love endures forever.*
> to him who struck down the firstborn of Egypt
> *His love endures forever.*
> and brought Israel out from among them
> *His love endures forever.*
> with a mighty hand and outstretched arm;
> *His love endures forever.*
> to him who divided the Red Sea asunder
> *His love endures forever.*
> and brought Israel through the midst of it,

His love endures forever.
but swept Pharaoh and his army into the Red Sea;
His love endures forever.
to him who led his people through the wilderness;
His love endures forever.
to him who struck down great kings,
His love endures forever.
and killed mighty kings—
His love endures forever.
Sihon king of the Amorites
His love endures forever.
and Og king of Bashan—
His love endures forever.
and gave their land as an inheritance,
His love endures forever.
an inheritance to his servant Israel.
His love endures forever.
He remembered us in our low estate
His love endures forever.
and freed us from our enemies.
His love endures forever.
He gives food to every creature.
His love endures forever.
Give thanks to the God of heaven.
His love endures forever.

On a night when He knew He would suffer for our sake, before the story you may know by heart of Christ betrayed and all the events that led to His death, before He was tied and whipped and bore our sins, before the cross, Jesus *paused*. He stilled in order to sing of enduring love. The kind that lasts forever. The kind found in the same breath that spun the stardust. The kind of love extended to me and you. He sang of the deeds of God, of His faithfulness, of His love never failing. This is why we still sing today and why we know, as Paul tells us in 1 Corinthians 14:26, that everyone "has a hymn"[3] and that when we gather together today, just as He instructed the early church in Ephesus, we must "Be filled with the Spirit, addressing one another in psalms and hymns and spiritual songs, singing and making melody to the Lord with your heart."[4] It's how we are supposed to care for one another, how we encourage, how we remember, how we speak into the thin, broken places in our own hearts, and how in those thin, broken places others share with us. When we pause and sing, we can call forth what God is creating and affirm our coming home. We sing a lullaby that stills our souls to hush and trust. A lullaby that feels familiar because it's the tune we were meant to always know by heart. We sing the gospel over one another, again and again, and it draws us in as brothers and sisters.

When Love Was Delivered Alongside the Electric Bill

I fiddled for my mail keys in a bit of a rush. Sweet Lael, just four years old, was by my side, antsy to be back at home as I balanced my bags and carried her scooter in the crook of one arm. Free of her burdens, she leapt into the elevator without me just as all our letters and catalogs spilled out onto the floor—and then, the doors shut with only Lael inside. I watched the light above the closed doors track her course up to our apartment above. I flailed to scoop up the mail, still a pile on the lobby floor.

Second floor . . . third floor . . . fourth . . . fifth . . . sixth. It had stopped. Phew. Thankfully, she had known which button to push, which number would lead her home. I waited for the elevator to return to the lobby and took in a long breath as I closed my eyes. *I'm almost at the apartment. Almost there.* I shuffled through the letters of the day: bills, more bills, a coupon from a local grocery chain, and then something I'd missed in my first pass of sweeping paper off the floor. A small envelope bearing my name, written in delicate calligraphy, caught my attention. I opened it immediately. A skyline of the city was sketched at the top along with a classic yellow cab. My heart lifted as I soaked in the verse written:

> Strength and dignity are her clothing and she laughs at the time to come. She opens her mouth with wisdom, and the teaching of kindness is on her tongue.[5]

Beneath it were the words, "I see this in you, Kristen! I love you." A song of encouragement from a sister. My friend Kari Jo has a ministry of words. She is a woman of truth and a woman of the Word, of hospitality and beauty but also of letters. The script of her hand is so lovely that she is often hired by large corporations to design invitations or paper details for swanky events. She is an artist at heart, and she brings love to paper. But the most beautiful works I've ever seen her create are on small cards slipped in the post to light up the hearts of her friends. I know I am not alone in receiving them. She sings truth on mad-dash days. These are the reminders of gospel song that helped release my own voice from fear and discord, placing it back in a divine melody. It was as if my heart rose with the elevator, from floor to floor, because my friend had encouraged me. An everyday moment of opening the mail had been made holy by her intentional love and friendship.

In fact, daily life and endeavors have always been a vehicle for the Psalms. Throughout the life of the early church, the singing of psalms continued, and we find the practice in worship mentioned in the writings of early church fathers like Tertullian and St. Jerome. Sometime during the latter part of the fourth century, St. Jerome recorded, "In the cottage of Christ all is simple and rustic, and except for the chanting of the Psalms there is complete silence. Wherever one turns the laborer at his plow sings Alleluia, the toiling mower cheers himself with Psalms, and the vinedresser while he prunes his vine sings one of the Psalms of David."[6] Everything was rustic, simple—except for the songs of Scripture, heaven meeting earth, Christ meeting His people as they strained in daily endeavors. As monasteries sprung up, psalms became a centerpiece in the daily rituals of Benedictine monks who would sing them as they gathered together eight times a day to sanctify the hours with prayer. To *sanctify* means to esteem, to make much of, or to make holy, and again, it is in these moments that heaven was ushered in, and where the psalms led lips to make way for Christ.

In Protestant tradition too, psalms became a central focus of liturgy, the order of worship in the church, both corporately and devotionally for each individual. In the *Book of Hours*, or the *Book of Common Prayer*, like the copy that's sitting even now with its rust-red binding on my coffee table, psalms are set before the Christian each day as a part of the daily readings. The original Psalter was often sung in designated meters and patterns after the Reformation, but then, Sir Isaac Watts revived devotional psalm singing into a model most of us are familiar with today. In 1719, he published a poet paraphrase of biblical psalms called *The Psalms of David* that included modern day hymns we still sing like "Joy to the World"[7] and "Oh God, Our Help in Ages Past."[8]

The Prayers of Christ through His Church

When I was growing up, our little Bible church used to meet at the old Grange Hall with its stripped-down, simple wood floors and kitchen full of mauve Formica. Most of my memories involve setting up and taking down metal folding chairs and singing together as a family alongside other children and their parents. Most of my friends went to other churches that had Sunday schools with snack bars and puppet shows, with tickets earned and then redeemed at a prize box full of neon plastic from the dollar store. They didn't sit with their parents, and sometimes, in my cold metal folding chair on Sunday morning, I daydreamed I was with them.

But in that gathering, I learned to sing hymns. I learned to sing words and truths that even to my young heart, sank gospel-deep. I learned how to belt out the promise that was yet unknown to me. Psalms and hymns like these teach us to pray in freedom and in feeling, but they also bring a form to our hearts, our words, and our voices. Like the meter shaped the music of the Psalter in congregations, psalms shape our prayers.

When we pray and sing the psalms, we are praying Scripture, and we find ourselves immersed in the Word and in the *mystery* of the Word. The words I pray and sing are the same words that accompanied King David as he danced, and that accompanied the lament of Israelites in exile. They are the prayers of a people returning home, rebuilding the temple and remembering the exodus at Passover season after season. They are the songs of the early church, echoing in rooms where the letters of Paul were read for the first time and in the catacombs under Roman rule and persecution, when brothers and sisters were cast before lions. These words rang out in cathedrals and then chapels and over waves to new worlds. Through wars and weddings, griefs and victories, the Psalter has been a companion to the people of God and is knit into the fabric of my own—of your own—history and heritage.

Most incredible to me, though, is that at one moment in our history, was a moment that gives gravity to all others, as the Word of God became flesh:

> In the beginning was the Word, and the Word was with God, and the Word was God. He was with God in the beginning. Through him all things were made; without him nothing was made that has been made. In him was life, and that life was the light of all mankind. The light shines in the darkness, and the darkness has not overcome it.[9]

Who was the Word? Who was with God in the beginning? Through whom were all things made? Who is life and the light of all mankind, shining in the darkness, not overcome? In one of the most profound sections of the Gospels, we learn that the *Word* is Jesus. It is remarkable, isn't it? Glory put on skin and as the eternal, divine Son of God walked the earth in our midst. The apostle John introduces us to Him as the Word. And we know that He prayed the Word, too. He prayed the Psalms. The Word, now dwelling in us, prayed the Word aloud while dwelling among us. As we also pray the Word, as we pray the Psalms and all the rest of Scripture, this is the mystery and the reality of the person and power of Jesus. As Dietrich Bonhoeffer wrote, "the Psalms are the prayers of Christ through the mouth of His Church."[10]

What does it mean when we pray in Jesus' name? When we come before God and beg for our hearts to align with His will in all our circumstances, when we determine that the truth of God's Word—the richness of all He has given to us in the Scriptures, and not the scarcity of our own souls—will determine the content of our prayers. In the psalms we encounter the prayers of the Word, in the Word, and He guides our heart to Himself by His Word. Bonhoeffer continues,

> Jesus Christ prays through the Psalter in his congregation. His congregation prays too, the individual prays. But here he prays in so far as Christ prays within him, not in his own name but in the name of Jesus Christ. He prays, not from the natural desires of his heart, he prays out of the manhood put on by Christ, he prays on the basis of the Man Jesus Christ. . . . This is what Scripture means when it says that the Holy Spirit prays for us, that Christ prays for us and in us, that we can pray aright to God only in the name of Jesus Christ. We should pray in faith the whole prayer of Christ.[11]

Jesus meets us tangibly in prayer. He is our companion, our intercessor, our intermediary. We can approach our home in God *through* Jesus, from the heart of Jesus.

In all my cries and in all my honest conversation with an intimate Creator who invites me to be near, I become aware that subtly, my heart has transformed before Him. Where I was once so desperate simply to speak, to pour out every bruised thought and ragged feeling, I'm finding now that my thoughts and feelings have changed their tune, have found their rhythm in an altered meter. I don't want my prayers to remain a repetition of my griefs; I don't want them to be about *me* at all. The more often I run toward Christ's arms and firmly embrace Him, the more I find that what was once clamorous is replaced with harmony. Misery is traded for praise. I come to desire that only the prayer of Jesus would remain. That His song would become mine, too, woven together, my words hidden in His. This is where I find *selah*—the rest for my soul painted there in the ink of the psalms' script. What if the connection of allegory and of reality, of music and of silence, of energy and of rest were all pairs that could truly meet—not in tension, but in true harmony? In Christ, there is a purpose and a place for all the in-betweens of my own life. *Selah* is an interlude between all these notes and mysteries. It is where the Word of heaven and the Word alive in me are found in Jesus, and when I embrace His beauty as my own, my heart finds peace. It is the only way my heart finds peace.

I pulled out a notecard from my stationery set. The crinkly white paper was frayed at the edges but smooth in the middle so I could draw out the loops of letters with my pen. A friend across the country had texted that she was discouraged and confused. I knew she needed to know that she was not alone, and although when I began to write, I wasn't sure what to say, the words tucked into my own heart from moments spent in Scripture began to curl out onto the paper:

> You are so beautifully and wonderfully made. I see such light in your eyes, such compassion in the way you listen, such care in the tasks you put your hands to. Do you know

> how you are loved and appreciated? Do you know that I love being your friend? Thank you for letting me see God's work in your life up close. Thank you for trusting me with your heart . . .

As I addressed the envelope and placed the stamp in the corner, I prayed, *Lord, let this note fill the rush of my friend's life with heaven. Let her feel Your heart for her in these words. May Your melody become her song.*

CHAPTER 8

Practicing Selah

Everybody needs beauty as well as bread, places to play in and pray in, where nature may heal and give strength to body and soul alike.

JOHN MUIR, *THE YOSEMITE*

As spring began to blossom in the city, I followed the moss and the bright green vines like a treasure map. They led me to the reservoir. In the dusk, I approached and took in the blue beyond the waist-high iron fence. I began to walk, and then to run. My feet scuffed the gravel as the sun set behind the towers on my corner in strips of violet and tangerine. I pushed my body around those two miles while the yellow globes of the street-lights flickered on all over the city, reflecting in the surface of the water. Their tones turned honey and green in the blue and gray shadows that emerged beyond them in the twilight. I could hear the cadence of my breath, a whir and then a hush as I exhaled, soft and free. My feet fell in rhythm with the beat of the music in my headphones. In and out, with focused breath, inhaling the lush scent of rain, the perfume of the blooms lining the trail. As

I breathed out, I could imagine I was soaring; although gravity's grip kept me at a slow pace, the sweat came as refreshment. I was keenly aware of the tension of fighting to move, to take more ground with every pad of my foot, and as I did, the stress of the day subsided, the strain in my body relaxed.

There was a rhythm to these runs that was sanctuary. A *selah* interlude.

Other evenings I'd pedal my bike through the lanes of Central Park. The assigned lane for cyclists hugs the lane for horses, and one day, as carriages full of tourists passed me, my face brightened with the realization that I *lived* here; I could take in the wonder every night. I swerved through the turn where my Lael, just a year before, had flattened her body on the pavement, tired and overstretched, refusing to go another step. She'd plastered her cheek against the cement, exhausted. She was only four then and didn't know she was in danger on the bike path, only that she could no longer lift her small legs. The weight of her body in the hot sun had become too much. As I kissed her cheeks and lifted her up onto my shoulders, I'd wondered if I could ever make this place home, or if my life here would ever be anything more than just trying to keep my people alive, actively thwarting danger and attempting to maintain our energy in this overwhelming city.

Now that I was out on the trail alone, I had time to take notice of a group of college students with yoga mats, a community cycling group, a woman jogging with her golden retriever. I felt a part of their winsome gathering. We were connected by our movement, each one of us fighting for activity that would refresh and strengthen us.

How many times have I tried to find strength all by myself?

How many times have I crashed and burned just like my girl Lael, flailing and feeling unable to go on? Too many times to count. We all need a coach, a friend, a trainer, a team—people who will root for us to break plateaus and to keep going when we think we can't.

One of my other favorite ways to exercise is through barre classes, a combination of ballet, Pilates, and yoga. The first class I ever took was an hour long, full of other students on mats and lined up at the ballet barre beside me. I focused on each of the steps, how the exercise affected my muscles and made my breath even, and before I knew it, it was time to cool down and head back home. My studio offered classes online too, prerecorded instruction you could tap into from anywhere, and when my schedule was crunched, I decided to give one a try instead of hauling myself out of the apartment. Twenty minutes in, I was done. I couldn't go any further. The movements I had mastered in class, that had challenged me but that I had accomplished were heavy and out of sync in my living room. I felt total fatigue come over me and turned the computer off. My discipline, my ability to break through mental and physical challenges was greater when I was working alongside others. Just like my running and biking in the park. The people who surrounded me on the trail didn't all share the same fitness regimen, but we were stepping forward, each in our own way, in a shared space. That we had in common.

When I walked in the door of our apartment after my run that night, I tiptoed out to the terrace and did my best not to wake the children. Josh and I had worked out a pattern for these nights when I'd run or cycle: We'd eat together as soon as he got home from work, and then I'd head out the door to catch the last bit of sun while the children helped him tidy up and got ready for bed. I usually made it back just in time to tuck them in with stories and a kiss. Sometimes, as on this night, their eyes were already heavy, or they were fast asleep. The sun had set and the deep blue of the sky had turned into indigo. From our perch, we could see that the skyline held thousands of sparkling stars, not visible in the heavens above, but the reflections of lamps and open windows shining out from the buildings that lined block after block. Chimneys and dormers peeked from the shadows and formed waves in mid-air, a community of high-rise dwellers invisible from the street below.

True rest is transcendent. It is a "seeing through," an icon, a reminder. In rhythm and in breath, in the physical and in the tangible objects of home and in the refreshment of my spirit, I was learning that *selah* was rest; it was pause and stillness. But as I sat, hushed, on our terrace, reflecting on all the exertion out there that I'd felt a part of that night, I realized I was beginning to understand that real rest isn't always idle. Sometimes rest is a full stop, but often it requires action: yielding, redirecting, trusting. Sometimes rest is a dance or a paced run through the park, even a slow lap around the pond. Sometimes resting means moving. Counterfeit rest, the kind offered on the cheap, is almost always passive. I need not receive from it, and its presence leaves no mark, no imprint of holiness or grace upon me. I can turn to Netflix for this kind of false rest, but even after hours of taking it in, I am left wanting. I may feel full and even tired after scrolling through social media, but I lack nourishment, like my belly when I pile in kettle chips and dark chocolate, or guzzle soda so that my stomach feels bursting and fizzy. Being bloated isn't the same as being filled (and the burping isn't pleasant for anybody.)

When I'm Squeezed

A teenage girl, unmarried and poor, was expecting a baby. She knew her circumstances would likely cause her to face the harsh gossip of neighbors and friends, that she might lose their company, her own stability, and her reputation. To anyone looking from the outside, her situation must have looked dire. But this teenage girl was Mary, Christ's mother. Even as she faced a future she did not understand, Mary responded with a song of praise. She said to the angel who greeted her with the news that she would become a mother, "Behold, I am the servant of the Lord; let it be to me according to your word."[1] She was willing. Her heart's posture was one of obedience and trust. And then, she continued with a prayer often referred to as the Magnificat or *Mary's Song*:

> My soul magnifies the Lord, and my spirit rejoices in God my Savior, for he has looked on the humble state of his servant. From now on all generations will call me blessed; for he who is mighty has done great things for me, and holy is his name. And his mercy is for those who fear him, from generation to generation. He has shown strength with his arm; he has scattered the proud in the thoughts of their hearts: he has brought down the mighty from their thrones and exalted those of humble estate; he has filled the hungry with good things, and the rich he has sent away empty. He has helped his servant Israel, in remembrance of his mercy, as he spoke to our fathers, to Abraham and to his offspring forever.[2]

Mary's heart was filled with Scripture. In her prayer she quoted Psalm 103 and Hannah's hymn, found in 1 Samuel 2:1–10. Her response to the angel's news is steeped in the knowledge of Hebrew Scripture that she had tucked away in her heart. She was full of faith, full of vision for God's mercy to His people, of His character and promises. When she faced uncertainty, everything she had invested in was reflected in her response.

Whatever you invest yourself in will be reflected in your soul. When I am squeezed, the contents of my heart will spill out. If I actively choose to invest in rest, in trust, in kindness, to sow these qualities intentionally into my life, to saturate my mind in Scripture, to actively engage the person of Jesus, I can offer those things to other people. But if I have a barren soul, if my internal life is void, if inactivity and leisure are my only occupation, then I will have nothing to give.

What do you take in, invest yourself in, as rest and nourishment so that you are able to pour it out? I made a list of things that stirred me and began to create a plan for how to incorporate a bit of each one, little by little, into my life:

- Baking with the kids
- Pouring tea in the afternoon
- Reading poetry
- Reading the Sunday paper
- Coffee with a friend
- Night walks under the stars
- Writing out Scripture
- Hand lettering
- Knitting
- Practicing my German
- Oil painting
- Watching old movies
- Listening to jazz
- Embroidering

- Writing letters
- Reading travel memoirs
- Walking through the galleries at the Met
- Planting herbs
- Making treats for our neighbors
- Arranging flowers
- Reading mysteries

I began to line my terrace with candles. I thought I could begin by offering up rest to my family at mealtimes, when we were naturally gathered together. Every evening as dusk dimmed the kitchen table, I lit long tapers to welcome my family into evening's song. We pulled out linen napkins and set each place with silver. My littlest helped me fill the water glasses. Even in winter we'd find small buds to display as a centerpiece. We prepared a place for warmth and rest, a feast together to pause in the brightness of our table and our meal. So unlike my early years of homemaking, when I'd pursued perfection as I set out dinner, now serving breads and mixing sauces began to feel like art, brimming out of the overflow of what was stored up in my heart. In all the details of our meals, I began to see that I was offering a haven. There was something holy in the way we set the table. It was its own *selah*, a resting place and shelter for my family and our friends, where we could join to inhale flavors and scents like rosemary and apple cider and sweet potatoes. Our hearts would spill out at our shared table as we freely shared our words.

When I folded flannel sheets and slipped a chunky throw over the arm of our sofa, I took in their textures as grace, as invitation to stop and breathe, to sink in and get cozy. Small encounters with artistry began to form a new pattern in my mind. The more I looked for *selah*, the more I beheld it, the more I cultivated it, the more I had to share.

CHAPTER 9

When We Miss Eden

For if we take the imagery of Scripture seriously, if we believe that God will one day give us the Morning Star and cause us to put on the splendour of the sun, then we may surmise that both the ancient myths and the modern poetry, so false as history, may be very near the truth as prophecy.

C.S. LEWIS, *THE WEIGHT OF GLORY*

Earth's crammed with heaven,
And every common bush afire with God,
But only he who sees takes off his shoes;
The rest of us sit round and pluck blackberries.

ELIZABETH BARRETT BROWNING, "AURORA LEIGH"

"Good morning, David,"

I rushed through a hello with my doorman as I pressed the children's' shoulders though the lobby and out to the sidewalk.

"Oh, package for you, ma'am."

I couldn't sign for it. I couldn't stop—we were late!

"We'll grab it when we get back home," I called back to him, my voice trailing behind me as I rushed down the steps that led to the street.

"Morning, Miss Kristen, those children are looking quite fine today!"

"Oh, thank you," I sputtered back to our neighbor as I continued to move forward without even making eye contact. It was 8:15, too late to walk five blocks to catch the subway, but Lael had left her scooter upstairs so we'd be too slow to walk.

"Okay, kids, we're taking a cab. Head to the corner!"

I shouted instructions for them to be cautious weaving around the other pedestrians and the line of students waiting to enter their classrooms in the private school adjacent to our building. *Oof!* Jones had already careened into another mother. I brushed past her, apologizing for his speed, and she gave me a knowing smile, likely having just finished her own morning sprint. We reached Central Park West, and Maia was already standing on the curb with her hand outstretched, looking for a taxi with its light on, ready and able to stop for our crew. I did my best to look a little disheveled and a little sad, hoping my expression might inspire a driver's pity.

As I tried to slow my heartrate and adjusted my sunglasses, a flash of kelly green caught my eye. Across the street, moss and ivy seemed to have sprung up overnight, a blanket of spring veiling the brownstone, and a welcome harbinger of a new season.

Winter had melted and warm days had begun to stick around, stretching out in rays of sunlight. I found myself staring. *Stop and listen,* it seemed to say.

Just below the vines, our favorite street vendor, Billy, spotted me and waved. Right now his business was all bagels, but this afternoon he'd greet my children and all the others from the neighborhood with kosher hotdogs and lollipops, passing them out like the Pied Piper and indulging my littlest by calling her "the Princessa."

"Moooom! We got a cab! Come on! Billy will still be here when we get home!"

I asked the driver to pop the trunk and threw in our scooters and backpacks before making my kids slide in, four of us across the back seat, Lael hopping onto my lap as I barely squeezed the door shut.

We won't be able to fit into a car like this for much longer. Should we think about buying a car? No, *I just need to be more organized, wake earlier, simplify our lives so we can always walk . . . what if we laid out our clothes the night before?* What *if I planned to buy lunches at the bodega and stopped trying to make them from home? Would that be too expensive?*

Just like that, I was tempted to forget about the ivy and dive back into my cluttered mind. But for just a moment, I *had* lingered. I'd borne witness to green against so much gray. And though it had only lasted a short moment, the reminder of that beauty sustained me all day. My soul had stopped racing when I looked full into the green, and I'd almost forgotten all the worries I'd been carrying of being late, all the to-dos I'd been checking off, all the ways I'd been stretching myself across the things that urgently needed my attention *right now.* A peace had risen to the surface of my mind and heart—and I wanted it to remain.

I'd had an interlude. A period of time, however brief, set apart from the natural pace, like in a piece of music, another kind of tune played in between verses or bars. *Selah,* that single word that held so much meaning and brought me to ponder rest and pause, is also translated and sometimes actually written in English translations of our Bible, as *interlude.* Interlude was another aspect of rhythm, a dance partner that would cut into your life and and whisk you away. It was the enchantment of escape that I could daydream about on busy days. For me, interlude had always looked like vacations and coffee hours and the places where beauty parlors resided. But when I thought of rest this way, it seemed like running after diversions and luxuries. I didn't want to merely chase the charm offered by this kind of rest in the midst of gray days.

On any given Saturday, our family would head out to hike or go on a nature hunt. We'd become experts at taking night walks through Central Park, under the canopy of the trees where we'd listen for raccoons, spy the waning slices of the silver moon, or gather the flame-colored leaves scattered on the ground in autumn. In paint plastered on walls and canvas in museums, in the cello echoing through Carnegie Hall or the ballerina's *arabesque en pointe* during the Dance of the Sugarplum Fairy at Lincoln Center, we'd *ooh* and *aah* and try to absorb each gift in the moment. Beyond these local excursions, I planned my two-week vacations like everyone else in our society, planned to hold them tight and soak them all in and try, oh just try, to keep finding a soul-filling something around the edges of my everyday in the meantime.

But I didn't feel at peace with cordoning off everyday life to grab at a rest that was wholly disconnected from regular rhythms. Is that what was meant to sustain us? Was this simply the way it was, the pattern we followed, crying out for the weekend and departure from the ordinary with the rest of our culture? Bemoaning the work week and mundane tasks and plotting and planning our getaways? Setting apart restful days was necessary to be sure, but I began to realize that I'd been confusing the bigger picture of rest with escape. I didn't want to keep living my life while always looking to flee it, satisfied only when I embraced recreation. I wanted *selah* to cut into the ordinary like it had just before I jumped into the cab that morning, because if rest had the potential to be perpetual, to be knit into my actual everyday life, it could transform all that was common into anything but. It could reshape the posture of my whole heart.

Interludes on the Upper West Side

Friday mornings had become my most beloved time to practice *selah*. I'd scrimped enough in our budget to hire a college student to come and spend a few hours helping homeschool the children while I slipped out to meet women from our neighborhood for Bible study and prayer. No matter the weather, I sauntered slowly for ten blocks to reach them, a steaming Café Americano in hand, my thoughts all my own. One day I walked by the hardware store and smiled at Izzy as he greeted patrons at the front door. On our first visit to his store, to purchase a plunger, he'd given each of my kids a silver dollar as a welcome to the neighborhood. My grocer was outside too, setting up the day's displays. He stopped to get my attention, telling me new raspberries had arrived and that they were glorious. He promised to set some aside for me, along with his wife's homemade baklava. He knew my sweet tooth couldn't resist.

I kept moving down Columbus Avenue and waved a greeting to our veterinarian's receptionist through the office window. As I approached our church, I took a deep breath, feeling expectant. I was gathering with women who were so very different from me in age and life circumstances, but we were united by the grace of meeting together. Our backgrounds and philosophies were many, but as we pondered Scripture together, as we worshiped and prayed, it was with one spirit, one heart and one affection: Christ.

On my way home that day, I weaved through side streets I'd rarely explored to stretch out my time. A red door on an old stone church creaked open as a parishioner walked out, and the sweet aroma of incense wafted into the street for just an instant. I spied candlelight inside beyond the empty pews. In church history, red doors are a sign of welcome, did you know that? For centuries, red doors have marked holy places as refuge and safety. Red doors welcome reconciliation and healing and pronounce an invitation. And I did feel welcomed in, perhaps because candlelight flickering on my own table spoke welcome and rest in our home, an invitation to sit, to eat, to be known. And now, this new table, this new sanctuary beckoned me to be known too. I slipped in and sat beside a pillar near the back. The shards of color in a stained-glass window above the altar shone red and blue, a cross hung before me, archways and columns surrounded me from beside and above, and still the fragrance of burning perfume filled my nostrils. It warmed me as I inhaled, enjoying the flickering sheen of candlelight. All my senses were alert in this place, down to my fingertips tracing the grain of the warn pew. There was delight in the aesthetics, but also an echo of holiness, of heaven. I was drawn to release my burdens. To pray. To become wholly and completely vulnerable. To meet. To practice *selah*. Interlude was the rest that I was going to embrace as I let go of all I was holding.

This attraction to beauty had to be named. I knew I was designed to be a partaker and a maker of this kind of light, and in the small and the simple, as my tensions released freely before God in this place, my heart was re-oriented to the One who is Rest; the one who is Beauty, and whose beauty could transform the very shape and curve of my life.

Why did light flickering or music dancing or the color green take my breath away so? These glimpses of beauty were also glimpses of grace, and the more I saw them, the more I wanted them, craved them. C. S. Lewis wrote in his essay *The Weight of Glory*, "We don't want to merely see beauty . . . We want something else which can hardly be put into words—to be united with the beauty we see, to pass into it, to receive it unto ourselves, to bathe in it, to become a part of it. . . . It is not the physical objects that I'm speaking of, but that indescribable something of which they become for a moment, the messengers."[1]

Beauty was what my soul longed for, what it hungered for. But more than beauty itself, I wanted to trace this beauty *back to its source*. The source was what I really wanted. Shadows of glory were showing me the presence of God in my midst and revealing the Sabbath world to me in murmurs. It whispered its presence in great art and carved stone, in watercolor and fresh lilies, in sunsets and evening tide, in fresh lemon and parmesan and butter sauce. The echoes of Eden breathed into a dry and weary world and called out to dry bones to wake and to walk,[2] to taste and to see what was good and right and lovely,[3] to keep the feast.[4]

Homesickness

One of my favorite movies is *Midnight in Paris*. It's about a writer who is struggling to tell a story, and one night while he's out walking, he falls out of time and into a community of artists during the 1920s. Ernest Hemingway, Gertrude Stein, the Fitzgeralds, and even Picasso become his compatriots. They who were once his idols, giants to him, are now his friends, inspiring and speaking into his work. Among them he finds his voice and his own perfect Paris, in a past he had always dreamed to make present. His homesickness for the ideal is satisfied there. Then, one evening, he falls even further back in time to the 1800s. The woman he connects with there is captivated by a carnival, by gas lamps, and by the style and poetry of her own just-out-of-reach perfection of time and place and *her* ideal Paris. And it is there that you realize both are pining for a way back, each by degrees in time, to ideals that will never pacify them completely. What they really desire—what we all desire—is to be one step closer to Eden. They yearn for an era that holds a promise they believe has evaporated with time, to be one step closer to their true home.

I've always wanted to go home again. I still dream about my bedroom at age eight, all periwinkle blue and white with Beatrix Potter wallpaper and my collection of ceramic bunnies lined up on the windowsill. Leyland trees lined the length of an entire fence in our yard. In the hollowed groves that ran between them, I'd construct a hall of rooms, each with a purpose, a giant dollhouse formed by evergreens. In my mind, their emerald needles touched the sky, and I felt swallowed up in the grandeur of the world I'd created.

A few years ago, some friends moved into a house across the street from my old home, and they lovingly secured an invitation from the current owners for my sister and me to revisit the place that held so many memories. As I approached the driveway, it was those Leylands off to the left that caught my eye first. They were nothing like I'd remembered. They weren't the same deep green; they had faded somehow. They were sparse. Thin. My brain scrambled to reconcile the house in my memory and the one that stood before me. *This was not my home.* I couldn't go in. I couldn't risk forfeiting more childhood memories to reality. I couldn't allow my sentiment to be undone.

Have you experienced this too? A returning to a place you hold vivid and sacred only to find it scarce and lacking? A neighborhood found cold, all the coziness gone from it? Your stomach drops. Hope flees. Nothing is as it should be, and it's as if this one moment displaces every memory you've treasured, every moment you've longed for, the remembered safety of your childhood home. Was any of it ever real? If the magic has gone from this place, then has it gone from all the rest? Our imaginations beg for nostalgia to be truth, for the evergreens of our youth to glow like they do in memory. Even if all our sentiments and ideals forever remain just out of reach.

In our first New York apartment, Helen had been our warden, our informant, and our friend. Her apartment was on the lobby floor of our building, so as you were coming in you would find her lying in wait, usually with cookies in hand or with news about a package, and often with an invitation to come inside and visit. Her walls were painted a deep emerald green with maroon trim. It was dark like a nightclub. I wondered sometimes if Helen had intentionally set the scene with evening lighting all day long, the kind that makes sunspots fade, that makes wrinkles and creases appear smooth—the kind of mood lighting that makes every woman feel like she's the brightest thing in the room. Mirrored bookshelves and dressers lined every wall, all piled with rows of photos in black and white and the occasional vase with real silk flowers. We'd spoken so many times, and yet I was always surprised by what I didn't know.

Central to most of her pictures was a young woman with a shock of platinum blond hair wearing a chic ball gown. On one particular afternoon, I realized she was posing with Frank Sinatra. I recognized his face first, but then began to realize the woman was squeezed in between other faces I knew: Dean Martin, Joey Bishop, Peter Lawford, and Sammy Davis Jr. *The Rat Pack*!

"Helen? Is this you?"

"Oh, of course honey, from the days when I sang at the Copacabana."

"You sang at *the* Copacabana?!"

Helen liked that I was surprised. I stared at the images of her in sequins, tried to imagine the buzz around her. With a croak in her voice, she told story after story about the legends she'd known so well. She spent a lifetime looking back and then looking out her window, to welcome people into her home and into her memories.

In many ways Helen reminded me of my own grandmother. Alone for nearly thirty years in the home where she'd raised her three girls, I'd almost always find her in her chair by the window when I arrived. Nothing there changed throughout my childhood. Although her girls had all left home, their rooms were untouched. She loved living in her memories and being surrounded by objects that comforted her and felt like old friends.

She planted red geraniums in her window boxes every spring. She prepared her pool so grandchildren could splash and cannonball, and piled plates high with peanut butter and jelly to feed us all afterwards. Each day she stared out the window at a tiny town she adored. When she spoke of it, she sparkled, but it was always in relation to what *had* been, never as it was in the present.

Helen, too, remembered the years she loved in her own way: tea in the eveninglike glow of her apartment, jazz playing on a record, stories of icons. Helen had years of health ahead, but she only wanted the past. She only wanted the Old New York, just as the writer in the film had wanted Old Paris, and just like my grandmother wanted her old little town in the mountains. In his book, *The Gospel in a Pluralist Society*, Lesslie Newbigin writes, "Nostalgia for the past and fear for the future are equally out of place for the Christian. He is required, in the situation in which God places him, to understand the signs of the times in light of the reality of God's present and coming kingdom, and to give witness faithfully about the purpose of God for all men."[5]

Do you see that longing for Eden is really yearning backward and forward all at once? We ache for Paradise past because it is the hint of our future promise, that we are all the time moving toward a new paradise. We live in the tension of an already here but not-quite-yet-arrived kingdom of God. When we have homesickness or heartsickness or desire to escape, to chase and consume more glitter, we must acknowledge its reality in us. But then we must determine its purpose in our lives. Is it merely a hum? A siren that sings from the past to call us backward to a world to which we cannot return? If that is the case, then we are very much at risk of following it right into the shallows and crashing like the sailors of *The Odyssey*. But if our homesickness is cause for us to look forward to a true and certain future hope, then we carry it with us as a foundation of our compassion, our ministry, and the light we bear to those around us.

At the Root of Our Longing

The famous author and philosopher Julian Barnes wrote, "I don't believe in God, but I miss him."[6] What does it mean to miss a God you don't believe in? Is it to hanker for an idea or to indulge in a wish? To wish God were real because then all the in-between, all the homesickness, the root of the chase for a future paradise would have a meaning? When we don't know that God has given us the desire for what has been lost as a means to find Him in the present, I believe that ache will have us looking for it anyway and anywhere. It's the reason we all vacation, the reason we long for loveliness and soak in experiences and people and words. We wish in the depths of all that we are for Eden and heaven to be true, for the trees to never lose their brilliance, for childhood haunts to retain a sense of wonder, for the magic of stories to come to life and to be certain.

But what if they are?

What if the magic of Camelot and the courage of knights fighting dragons and true love's kiss are all true? What if Verdi's *Requiem* rings thundering as nonfiction, proclaiming the heart of true heroes and victors? What if the sonnets of love are the surest language of the universe? The friendship of Frodo and Sam, the passion of Juliet and her Romeo, the dance of the waterlilies at Giverny and the spirals of *Starry Night* . . . what if they are more real, more constant, more present than anything else in our line of sight? All because they point us toward how we were truly meant to live and to a grandeur that surpasses them all, known only in Christ? If earth's crammed with heaven, then our home forever is here too, held in our hearts. When we pray as Jesus taught us, "thy kingdom come . . . on earth as it is in heaven," He guides us before the Father to usher in that kingdom *now.* To believe and to know that there are glimpses of light and color tucked into the darkness we see requires that we choose to bear light to others, to hold a lantern, to light a candle, to enter communities with the intention to shine. We live on the road home. In the tension of paradise past and future, we live in the waiting.

Interludes that woo us and beauty as we behold it are glimpses we are drawn to, but they are mere reflections. If we remain satisfied by their shadow alone instead of wondering what compels us to bow and barely lift our faces before we bow again, if we only allow only splinters of grace to move us, we miss true glory. It's easy to find peace with beauty that is comfortable to us, beauty that is only attractive to the eye. This is a distant kind of majesty that we are able to manage because it requires nothing from us except a pleasant gaze and enjoyment. But the beauty and light that transforms death to life, exchanges shriveling flesh for healed skin? That is a beauty we become subject to, a beauty that demands a reordering of our entire lives. As we fix upon it, we will find it wholly attractive and yet wholly terrifying. This is the moment when we realize that if we long for the lion of Christ to breathe life and create anew in us, we must draw close. We may find we echo the question of Susan, a future Queen of Narnia, when she asked, regarding Aslan, "Is he quite safe?" Across a table spread with toast and jam, dear old Mr. Beaver answered her affectionately, and he answers us as well, "Who said anything about safe? 'Course he isn't safe. But he's good."[7]

In 2 Peter, the apostle tells us what it was like to look upon the full glory and light of Christ on the holy mountain at the Transfiguration. But instead of pining for that moment, he tells the church to carry that light with them into the future. To "pay attention to it, as to a lamp shining in a dismal place, until the day dawns and the morning star rises in our hearts."[8] We must hold onto the light we have been given. Its beauty is haunting, a whisper not of what has passed but of what is to come. We are the forerunners now, bearing lamps to others and keeping a fire burning in our hearts until the Morning Star blazes within us upon His return. *Selah* interludes help me remember to keep the ember burning.

CHAPTER 10

Eyes to See

Gracious God, we confess that we have longed too much for the security of this world. We have loved the gifts more than the giver. In your mercy, help us to see that all the things we pine for are shadows, but you are substance; that they are quick sands, but you are mountain; that they are shifting, but you are anchor.

THE BOOK OF COMMON PRAYER

When I gazed at the stars as a little girl, so captivated by the vast sky, my little sister was swallowed up by the darkness. The stars were invisible to her. I remember much of first grade was spent in the waiting room of the doctor's office waiting for tests, taking trips to special hospitals and waiting again, laying out my colored pencils and lined paper on coffee tables next to a stack of magazines and slowly writing out my name to keep busy. I never understood the flurry of concern around me. Julie was diagnosed with a disease that had begun to rob her of sight, even as a preschooler. I began to hold her hand even when it seemed awkward, guiding her by the arm to our seats in a movie theatre or dimmed church. I still have to be sure to get right in her line of sight so that she doesn't have to pretend to see me off to the side, and to always remember to turn on extra lights when she enters a room.

Julie is a mother now. She glows with the love of Jesus and illuminates every place she occupies. She's still never seen the stars. But the eyes of her heart? They know how to imagine glory. The eyes, Scripture tell us, are "the lamp of the body. If your eyes are healthy, your whole body will be full of light."[1]

What comes over us when we are despairing in *spiritual* blindness? When not just a room, but the fabric of the whole world feels dim? Do we hide ourselves away? Do we minimize our need, harbor anger, or maybe keep working harder and longer to produce a sense of self-worth? Just like physical blindness shrinks what we take in through our eyes, spiritual blindness shrinks what is in our hearts and can stop us from walking in the grace and beauty of community. It can prevent us from living in thanksgiving, from noticing the kindness of doormen and hotdog vendors, from appreciating the intention in the brushstrokes of the masters or the tenor of the cello. When the eyes of our hearts are sick, we experience the plucking of a harp rather than the tune, the hurry in a crowd rather than the presence of our friends, hunger when we are seated at the banquet table rather than appreciation of the feast before us. But when our vision is healed, the beauty we've longed for revives us, because it points us to one the One who is our promise incarnate. When we wind *selah* into the regular days and rhythms of our life, we are knitting in the delight of God, the presence of God, and the gifts of God. We must first receive them. Then we must walk in them.

The Brightness of Glory

Sight came to the apostle Paul dramatically. Acts 8 opens just after the stoning of Stephen, after he had called out that he could see heaven open and the Son of Man, Jesus, standing at the right hand of the Father. As he died, he cried out on behalf of those who killed him, seeking forgiveness for those who had beaten him bloody until his life was snuffed out. Saul approved the killing. He had ravaged the church, dragging men and women from their homes. His very breath, Scripture tells us, exhaled murder.[2] But then, even as he sought to hunt down Christians on his way to Damascus, Saul was struck blind. He fell to the ground. Jesus was with him, speaking right to his heart. And while those with him heard the voice of the Lord too, Saul was the only one to *see* Him. Although his eyes were open, he was blinded by glory, and only after he was commissioned with the gospel and filled with the Holy Spirit did scales fall from his eyes, restoring his sight.

No one in Jerusalem believed he had become a disciple. No one could believe in that kind of change! But his face-to-face encounter with Christ altered him utterly and completely. His entire identity was made new, even his name. His letters and instruction, his faith, and his sacrifices all brought the song of hope, the gospel, to the Gentiles. He took the abounding and saving mercy of Jesus, known first in his own life, to all the nations and peoples he could reach.

Moses was a murderer too. He rushed ahead to seek his own method of justice in his own way in Egypt and killed a slave driver. Fear of the repercussions drove him into the desert where he stood on holy ground before the presence of God in a burning bush. He became compelled by his calling as the deliverer of his people, embracing the role tentatively amidst his own fears of inadequacy. When he came down from Sinai again with the Ten Commandments enfolded in his arms, he glowed: "His face was radiant because he had spoken with the LORD. When . . . all the Israelites saw Moses, his face was radiant and they were afraid to come near him."[3]

I've tried to imagine this kind of brightness, the illumination that flows from the presence of God, even the purple of His robe that fills the throne room of heaven. How could Moses bear to leave the sight of the Lord? How could he turn away and return to the ordinary?

Do you know that Scripture says the cherubim and seraphim are not able to leave the feet of the Lord? Of their own will, these creatures of heaven are in a state of ceaseless praise. As they look upon the Father, they are filled with such amazement, overcome by such majesty that they cannot help but fall to the floor again, bowing low in worship until they look up again at the presence of God and are driven once more to their knees. Forever beholding glory.

Receiving a Miracle

In the story of the exodus, God's people had just seen glory open wide and make a way for them. The sea split in two, torn right through for them to walk over sand and shells toward freedom. They were led by a pillar of fire in the darkness and a cloud hanging low in the light, guiding them toward a new home of God's making where they would be rooted in the promise of the covenant with Abraham. Living amidst miracles, having just seen the hand of God cover Egypt with plagues and even death for their benefit, one might assume their faith would be unshaken, thanksgiving ever present upon their lips, but it was hunger that endured.

While we are a part of humanity, the pang of our physical wants and need are never fully deferred. As the Israelites surged into the desert, taken over by hunger and thirst, a groan, a grumble grew from their gut. They feared they'd been left for dead, left alone. They complained and expressed fear, they had no trouble grieving for their captivity, preferring it over the desert of deliverance. As I read their story, I hear echoes of my own life in discord, my preference for noise over silence. But the presence of God was near to them as He was near to me. He who had extended a hand of rescue spoke to Moses when He heard the people's cries:

> Behold, I am about to rain bread from heaven for you, and the people shall go out and gather a day's portion every day, that I may test them, whether they will walk in my law or not. On the sixth day, when they prepare what they bring in, it will be twice as much as they gather daily." So Moses and Aaron said to all the people of Israel, "At evening you shall know that it was the LORD who brought you out of the land of Egypt, and in the morning you shall see the glory of the LORD, because he has heard your grumbling against the LORD.[4]

Despite their questioning of His Word and provision, despite their hearts curving inward, God didn't turn away until they were faithful; He didn't stall until they trusted in absolutes; He didn't wait until their lives were tidy and buttoned up. *He met them.* Scripture says their grumbling was *the reason* He poured out heaven.

When the manna fell to fill them, the Israelites were instructed to gather only a day's portion and nothing more. There was to be no tucking away of extras; only what they could eat that day alone. Instructions from God always hold a deeper meaning, leading us toward a greater flourishing. If they obeyed, they would know the One bending low to pour out provision and to dwell among them. Manna, God said, would show the glory of the Lord, so close that they could *see*. When I read of this, my head is often spinning, my eyes want to know, *What does glory even look like? Is it the same as the light on the road that changed Paul, the same awe that fills the cherubim and seraphim?*

We know that glory *dwelt* at Mt. Sinai. With a voice that quaked and a presence that burned fire in a bush, *it was heard*. We know that glory filled the tabernacle that was to come, that it pitched its tent to live among a beloved people. *It was felt.*[5] And we know that once, glory was clothed in flesh, to be with us and for us, and to be our very bread. *Glory put on skin.*

> And the Word became flesh and dwelt among us, and we have seen his glory, glory as of the only Son from the Father, full of grace and truth.[6]

I've often thought that seeing God's power would be all it would take to infuse someone's faith, to sustain their life for the long haul and bring forth change. Those who questioned Jesus often begged Him for miracles—they wanted a sign to prove He was the Son of God before they approached too near, and although Christ often performed wonders, more often He beckoned those with doubts to simply come to Him. To experience the mystery of knowing God with skin on: all the glory of heaven in the shape of a man among us. The power of God was *never* separated from His person.

When I look at Matthew 17, I think I'm quite a bit like Peter. He is always rushing forward, always looking at what is next, passionate and impulsive. Jesus took him, along with James and John, away from the other disciples. On a mountain, high, alone, and removed, the Bible tells us that Christ's "face shone like the sun and his clothes became as white as the light."[7] He was joined in that place by Moses and Elijah. Faced with the transfigured brilliance of his beloved friend and teacher, Peter doesn't fall to the ground like the seraphim and cherubim. He sees glory with his eyes, and he must busy himself—he doesn't sit and just behold Jesus, he works to find his place in the moment. He is quick to offer to build tents for the three men to dwell in. But then, *then*, the Father speaks. God interjects and starts to talk even as Peter is still grasping for worth with his words. He causes a hush to come over Peter's heart, as we see in Matthew 17:5–6: "And then a voice from heaven said, 'This is my beloved Son, whom I love; with him I am well pleased. Listen to him!' When the disciples heard this, they fell facedown to the ground, terrified."

This is the kind of Jesus I think we all want. The version of the Lord that, if they had seen Him, would clearly have caused all of Israel to bow before Him, to recognize Him, to love Him. This Jesus could have blazed through the politics and injustice of the day and brought a kingdom that would have immediately righted things on earth. But Jesus entrusts just these three disciples to see Him illuminated, to hear the voice of the Father proclaim His identity. Jesus then goes to His friends and touches them. He initiates. He tells them to rise, to have no fear. It's the personal, the intimate Jesus who convinces them to look up. When they do, they see only Him, standing with them, alone.

Peter's response before beholding the glory of the Lord in the transfiguration is drastically different than it is afterward. Peter longed to do something, to busy himself before something was done to him. In everything happening around him on that mountain, Peter was no longer central. He could not fill the silence with his words or actions; instead, Jesus filled the moment with *Himself*.

I feared silence like Peter because I felt it was my responsibility to fill it, and I settled into discord, allowed it to drone on, because it was the only noise I could muster alone. Music and melody are not something I am able to produce on my own; they are God-breathed and come only when He is directing the notes of my life. In *selah*, in true rest that cuts into our vulnerable prayers, into our lament, into our circumstances and courses, our focus becomes only Jesus. This is the catalyst of revival, of restoration, and of peace.

The words of the Father are what quiet Peter's heart. When he *really* sees Jesus, his whole life shifts. Likewise, when we see Jesus as He is, transfigured and divine, all interlude, all beauty, all desire makes sense. They have all along pointed to Him, transcendent in their purpose.

The true beauty we've wished to see, the glimpses of God we've longed for, are known fully in Christ. "The Son is the radiance of God's glory and the exact representation of his being, sustaining all things by his powerful word."[8] Jesus is the final word, the final breath, after the first. He is the ultimate revelation of God; there is no beauty beyond Him. Our relationship with Him begins because we find Him incomparably beautiful, but it is sustained because He is intimate with us, meeting us in interlude and *selah*. Modern day theologian and pastor Tim Keller said in a sermon one Sunday, "A sunset cannot replace a friendship or a marriage because as beautiful as it is, it is impersonal and we know that we have a personal God."

Why does a personal God matter? How does the fact that He is personal change us? In the profound transformations of Paul and Moses and Peter, they all came so close—face-to-face with God, they walked with a miracle, and they were never the same. When I am able to see God's glory, He is personal to me too, known to me, holding the strings of the universe together as He reaches to embrace me. As the prodigal son ran homeward, he was finally able to exhale in the arms of his father. Not because he had reached the end of his journey or saw the promise of his home waiting in front of him, but because he was enfolded by a person who loved him unconditionally. His rest, like mine, is personal, because it can only be known through a person. It is Christ who meets us. All our tension and all our peace are held by Him. The pause, the rest, the interlude is Jesus. *Selah* and Sabbath are a person.

How can it be so? Because Christ is not fully known when He is merely transfigured, but as He is crucified. All the whispers of true glory lead us to Calvary. In the calm before the storm of the Last Supper, the feasting after the foot washing, breaking bread, drinking wine, and establishing the reminder that He was with us, Jesus looked toward heaven and prayed, "Father, the hour has come; glorify your Son that the Son may glorify you."[9] God's glory was fulfilled in Jesus alone, in His broken body, in His death. In His suffering and sacrifice . . . for me. For you.

When Selah and Sorrow Meet

When Good Friday approaches, I usually enter church tentatively. Meditating on death, on the blood of the Son, the joy of God with us, His crushed bones, His dire thirst, I cringe and even recoil.

The Lord of the transfiguration was taunted by those who crucified Him: "See if Elijah comes for him," they mocked.[10] My heart longs to shout, "Elijah has come!" He has been wrapped in the illumination of heaven, under the affirmation of the Father bellowing approval in the covering of a cloud. And then, we read, with the memory of His Father's pleasure fresh but His face now turned away, Jesus expelled His last breath. The same breath that touched the stars and created the dance of the planets; that brought dry bones to life, shaping Adam out of dust; that kissed humanity into existence—in that moment it departed Jesus's battered body. The sorrow of death and the tomb can scarcely be recounted before I turn away too, so unsettled by this ugly beauty that requires something more of my heart, that requires all of me.

Holy Saturday is waiting for the resurrection. It was a wait that echoed through the whole earth. A wait that held the tension of all depravity and all hope together at once. It was the pause where all Creation held its breath, and where I find myself, year after year, holding tight to the reality that this interlude, this exchange of His life for mine, is *selah* incarnate.

I can expend my life chasing and finding pause, but if every rest, every yield, does not lead me here to this moment at the cross, then they are futile. I have succumbed as well to the fate Paul describes when he wrote to the Romans:

"For although they knew God, they neither glorified him as God nor gave thanks to him, but their thinking became futile and their foolish hearts were darkened. Although they claimed to be wise, they became fools, and exchanged the glory of the immortal God for images made to look like a mortal human being . . ."[11]

I want only a glory eternal.

CHAPTER 11

When We Fear Scarcity

No one ever told me that grief felt so like fear.

C.S. LEWIS, *A GRIEF OBSERVED*

A heat wave had turned the grass so thin and brittle that it crunched under my sandals. As I trod up the stone path, I let out a deep sigh. Even though the ground was parched and overgrown with thistles, my heart was tucked into this earth, into this cemetery.

My children ran ahead, bouquets in their small hands, ready to place them on the burial place of their baby sister. We'd never visited before, and I was anxious and curious about how much of the cemetery ritual would be understood. As they left my side, I mulled over who had laid these stones. Did they know as they labored that their hands were laying out a gift? When dirt rubbed into calluses and made its way under fingernails, did they recognize that they were making a way for mamas like me to grieve? Did they sense how I would never be able to touch these stones without catching my breath? I ambled up, walking on sacred tiles laid by healing hands, and rounded the corner to the Children's Garden—the infant graveyard, a gracious clearing for the babies and the unborn laid to rest. I listened as my eight-year-old read the names marked in stone. Even as my stomach lurched, I managed a grin, an attempt to display composure for Maia, so new to this place. I wanted her to be untroubled, unafraid, so in a place where tears usually flow freely, I choked mine back. I drove out sorrow in a space that aims to draw it out, a space for mothers like me who have buried the hope and promise that once grew unguarded in their swollen bellies, for those of us with hearts so full and arms so empty.

My girls, twirling in a circle around the flowerbed, abounding in life, in giggles, in innocence, struck me as a paradox in this graveyard. As I moved in closer to scoop them both up, to squeeze their cheeks and kiss the tips of their noses, I saw it: overshadowing a swath of purple, *a giant weed.* Something broke in me then and the tears began to flood. I trampled it, yanking at it, my face flushed in anger as more weeds entered my view. Tearing and hacking, I just wanted them gone. I was determined that there would be one less killer of life here, one less chunk of ugliness crowding out the lovely in this place. Protecting the flowers, the sentries of departed children, suddenly felt like the most urgent undertaking of my life, and as I weeded the garden, dirty at the knees, I screamed at the devil with my thoughts: *You will not choke out one more ounce of life today!*

In my frenzy, I barely noticed little feet appearing by my knees, little hands extending a bouquet of wildflowers, of life. The last bit of the day's light glowed steady behind the hills, and I calmed enough to remember the One who breathes beauty like this gently into my life. I wanted to know He was here. I imagined He'd been pulling the weeds a lot longer than I had. Once, He even sat beside the sea while multitudes gathered to hear Him talk of planting, of pruning, and of gathering:

> The kingdom of heaven may be compared to a man who sowed good seed in his field, but while his men were sleeping, his enemy came and sowed weeds among the wheat and went away. So when the plants came up and bore grain, then the weeds appeared also. And the servants of the master of the house came and said to him, "Master, did you not sow good seed in your field? How then does it have weeds?" He said to them, "An enemy has done this." So the servants said to him, "Then do you want us to go and gather them?" But he said, "No, lest in gathering the weeds you root up the wheat along with them. Let both grow together until the harvest, and at harvest time I will tell the reapers, Gather the weeds first and bind them in bundles to be burned, but gather the wheat into my barn."[1]

So weeds will appear, right along with the wheat until the very end—the tulips along with the cinder, the innocent laughter of my girls at the grave of my baby, the glory of the sunset spreading across etched tombstones. It all stands together until the One who will make all things right sees fit to do so. He is the constant gardener, aware of all the thorns encroaching sacred places. He knows the tensions, the fears, the doubts, the pulling of my body when it jerks, the pulling of my heart in different directions and different geographies as we struggle to make new places home. One day He will grab hold of it all, and when He pulls those weeds, they won't ever grow back. But me? I still struggle to believe it is true, to hold it as gospel in my everyday.

My fingers felt raw, pricked by the nettles, worn and numb, stains of dirt running through the folds of my skin, the muddy tracks where the earth had made its mark. My hands were aching and tired, but I wouldn't let go. I was still clenching blooms in one hand and weeds in the other, my grievances stacked up right alongside my gratitude.

I realized I'd been living like this for a long time, always placing gifts and burdens side by side on the scales, to weigh and measure. I'd despair that harvest might never come, wonder if the weeds were not simply the mark of an enemy and the consequence of a fallen world, but rather, an indication that God's goodness was scarce. My mind twisted as I considered, *Who but God could withhold life? Who but He could cause calamity? Did He not knit my womb and the children first formed there with purpose?* The worship of His name was fresh on my lips, but there was a hollow in my heart. I was hungry. My longing was to taste of the tangible goodness of God by knowing Him.

Distrust and unbelief always tug at what God has woven, threatening to cut us loose. Their whisper echoes in the ears of His daughters today as they whispered in the cool of the garden when they first rumored to Eve: *Does he really love you? Then why does he withhold the fruit that you can clearly see is good and pleasing? Why does he keep it just out of reach, taunting you with its perfume, but forbidding you to take hold and to taste? Eat what is good! Eat what you have been missing! Be filled by knowing! You want to know, don't you? You want to see.*

And so Eve ate. I've wondered if that first bite was bitter. Did it taste sweet upon her tongue before its flesh turned sour? When did she know; when did a deeper hunger set in? When did lost hope turn her sick? Eve, like I and so many others have done a million times since, chose to make her own way. She exchanged the glory of *knowing God* in order to know for herself, to find out if she could try to provide by her own strength what she feared God would never give.

Bread Within Reach

Blustery winds and snowfall were staples of my childhood winters in the west. A dreamy lull fell over the valleys after every dusting, crystals glistening on sidewalks and stoops, and families stayed tucked indoors to burrow by the blush of firelight. The quiet was always preceded by the buzz of preparation: laying out snowsuits and folding wool coverlets, stacking candles and matches and canned goods on the counter. I loved riding along with my mother on the final trip to the market before the flakes fell, saying hello to the crowds of friends and neighbors who were stocking up too. We were all in on the secret and ready for it together. When we'd finished unloading bags and filling the fridge, fitting new batteries into flashlights, and slipping on socks, my mother would look at me, childlike and cheerful and say, "Now doesn't that feel good, sweetie?" I don't think there is a woman alive who doesn't feel the comfort and satisfaction of a full cupboard and canned food to spare. We tend to have an appetite for a little extra, a little "just in case." There is nothing quite like being settled in and secure, never at risk for anything less than full.

We'd moved into our second New York apartment sight unseen. In all the photographs, the kitchen was the apartment's shining glory. One thousand square feet held three tiny rooms and two baby closets, so we'd filled the shower stall in the spare bathroom with boxes of folded sweaters, craft supplies, and Christmas tree ornaments. But that kitchen, oh, it was speckled with sea-blue tile and stainless-steel appliances. I was determined to bring it to life with recipes to nourish and warm our worn-out souls that winter. Racing against a February blast of sleet and snow, it wasn't until I returned from my first trip to the grocery store that I realized the truth: *it was all a lie.* The fridge shone tall and beautiful, but it was less than half the usual depth. The freezer? A measly rack of small drawers. I cried right there. We would make it all fit; we'd brave small trips to the corner bodega and learn to buy milk by the half gallon, but I couldn't shake the itchy need to be filled to the brim.

After I learned my refrigerator was a lie, there was more letting go, more spilling out, less room to store all the things. Old clothes tumbled out of the shower, tipped an empty car seat, and narrowly missed my five-year-old. We piled up our cast-offs and hailed a cab to haul them to a donation center twenty blocks away.

I didn't notice the penguin pajamas until I dropped the last box onto the curb, with the taxi waiting. They didn't belong in the bin at all; full of holes, they should have gone straight to the trash. But here they were, the pajamas I'd given my husband on the first Christmas Eve after we'd been married. Driving away, all the memories flooded back: the two of us, young, finding our way as we made a new life, foggy mornings of coffee and newspapers, pajama days snuggling newborns. I began to ugly-cry and begged the driver to turn back. I grabbed those pajamas off the top of the donation box right there on the corner, and I saw all the holes, saw the way time had eaten them through. I was sobbing on the street, the driver staring at me, tears falling because I was distraught at having to part with my rags. This was something more than just missing the past; this was me starving.

I read a study several years ago about people who had endured starvation and how it changed them.[2] The study revealed common traits in all the subjects. Even in old age, even when their days of hunger were long gone and their pantries were now full:

- They could never allow others to eat from their plates.
- Their bodies stood guard, their posture hovering and protecting their food.
- They were ready to defend their portion.
- They often binged, stuffing themselves beyond their capacity, beyond need.
- They could not fall asleep without bread within their reach.

These souls who had hungered, who had ached for relief and rest, needed to see bread *first* in order to rest. They had known the smart of emptiness, and they would fight to be full. They'd fight for the scraps and elbow loved ones aside for the last bite. In the meantime, they'd plow in excess, stir it thick, and gorge themselves rather than face the fear of life in a vacuum ever again. All kinds of emptiness, not just that of physical starvation, find us grasping later on. In the body or in the soul, we will cling to scraps if necessary, just so that we are holding on to something. We'd rather have scraps than nothing, the same way we'd rather have clamor instead of silence fear it.

I was afraid to find myself empty, unwilling to let go. Perhaps the weeds had won the day and I'd lost every bloom. I'd been weighing and measuring for so long, racking up the difference between grace and sorrow, I'd somehow forgotten that *all is grace.* When I felt goodness drifting, I realized that in my spiritual hunger, I'd started to assume that the God who knit me together might just let me unravel and stop giving. He might always keep the best fruit just out of reach. If I could gather it up like manna when it fell, I could tuck it away and be safe. But we know what happened to manna when it was stored away, don't we?

I longed to feel the satisfaction of a bulging fridge. It was my modern twist on gathering manna in the desert sun and trying to hoard it. I'd hoard my calendar too, fill it up to bursting busy to avoid quiet. With crowded schedules and teeming plates, stuffed rooms and overburdened lives, we pack ourselves full, yet we still feel empty. I began to notice carts at the grocery store piled high with everything in bulk, store rooms and garage shelves everywhere I went lined with extras. We don't want to rest unless we know good things are within reach, just like the bread on the night table. But what are we all really hungry for? What do we believe will actually fill us? It seems that the grumbling of our hunger has become a roar. Something deep in our bones remembers when we, the daughters of Eve, were met with that pang of loss in the garden, when we first felt a void. Now we are forever pining, trying to find our way back to being filled up, back to being whole.

Controlling Instead of Trusting

My children romped through Central Park on Tuesdays. We packed up lunch pails with neat rows of bread and jam, cucumbers and cream cheese. I set aside wool blankets to be draped over the Great Hill, a famous spot in the north of the park where you can see all the skyscrapers and where we'd meet up with friends each week. This was to be a haven for the mothers, where we would spread our feast and open our hearts while our children built fairy houses and mined for the gold of their imaginations among the clefts of rock nearby. The Hill always welcomed us to a quiet meeting. My body knew the respite that was coming, and I always had the funny sense that I was being drawn there.

But there was a pull on the other end of the string. Arguments flooded my apartment. I couldn't decide where to mop up first. Schoolwork was left blank, strewn alongside the crusts of toast and rinds of oranges on the dining table; chores were undone; there were messes everywhere. I was stretching toward the front door and our picnic, eager to take hold of the enjoyment that lie ahead, but my children were struggling to complete their chores. I bent low to train, to remind them of what we needed to accomplish, but their responses were not cooperative. Their legs ached to run *right now*, and their words clashed with mine before I could even speak them. We were all yelling then, piercing hearts and barking orders and crying out "I can't!" All I wanted to do was bounce back to find that center of beauty and rest, to the blanket laid out on the grass next to our friends, but I was stuck, standing as a hypocrite before tiny eyes and wounded hearts. Expectations for the day broke into fragments—and in my mind, I'd returned to the graveyard. I was trading beauty for bitterness. I was pulling the weeds again, and clenching them tight, fussing with every one, itching to control my days and my portion. I kept passing over the wheat that sustains while I gripped shriveled grasses instead.

When we did finally reach the park, my smile was plastic, my eyebrows high, my hello a sing-song. The children and I had struggled through the *I'm sorrys,* I'd hugged and kissed foreheads and we'd tried to move on, but the truth of the anger I'd expressed still hung in the air. I was afraid of being found out; I felt like a fraud as I smiled and pulled out sandwiches and goldfish crackers. I decided to tuck away all of the morning's painful moments. *I was covering up with fig leaves.*

When we don't perform well, when we fail or feel as if we've become a big ol' flop, when we've grieved so hard and felt so empty that we begin to grasp and control, our tendency is to hide. For me, it isn't all that different from the kind of mask I wore when I was afraid to bare my soul before God. This is my attempt to cover shame. Adam and Eve tacked fig leaves together, covering their nakedness as soon as they knew they were bare, as soon as their shame was out in the open.

I stitch my leaves together too. We all do. I spin excuses and give context, blame my circumstances, tell a white lie. When we are hiding, most of us would do anything to protect the exposed flesh. We wear a kind of worry, held tight, that whispers in our ear that hiding is all good and well, because . . . *If you knew the real me, you'd run. You'd recoil, with the same reaction that led me to stitch up a life of fragile leaves in the first place.*

When Adam and Eve hid, God called out. He came to find them. And even after all the penalties of sin had been dealt, He fashioned clothes for them out of animal skin. *Blood shed on behalf of humanity, to clothe shame.* The first death in the new creation was to cover them.

When the Israelites grumbled and complained, God met them too: He poured out manna to nourish their bodies and restore their hearts; His very presence was their food. And as for me, with all my anger, all my tensions churning and the fear I carried in my gut, *God met me.* He is always consistent in His response to those He loves. He is always drawing close, always wooing us to remember. *You are not naked, but clothed. You are not bound, but free.*

> I am the living bread that came down from heaven. If anyone eats of this bread, he will live forever. And the bread that I will give for the world, is my flesh.[3]

The apostle John recounts that when the crowds were aching for more loaves and fishes, even after baskets held the leftover weight of a miracle, they rushed after Jesus to follow their hope and their hunger. They chased Him across the water, where He told them He was the bread that had come down from heaven, and that *in Him* was the manna and every other good thing.

The Miracle of More

"They're here, they're here!" Jones and Lael ran to the door to greet their friends. It was Friday night, and everyone had plans. Maia emerged from the bedroom, cuddling her guinea pigs and giggling with her own friends who'd joined us after school. The bell rang again, and as the children swung the door open in excitement, our beagle spotted his chance for escape and dashed into the hallway. Halle heard me yelling after him and raced out the door with his leash.

"I've got him, Mom!" She exhaled and gave me a reassuring look, then offered to chase him down and walk him in Central Park before she left to meet friends to go out for the evening. The boys who were visiting had rushed in the door and were already turning on the Xbox while the younger girls ran to claim the terrace for a princess tea. This was how, in the course of a few minutes, three animals were in sight (one running between our legs), teenagers lined the hallway of our apartment in multiple directions, and little ones were squealing with delight in all the other corners. Josh knew the chaos had reached a tipping point. He opened the door to our bedroom—the only remaining quiet spot—and stuck his head out.

We could both feel every inch of our home's one thousand square feet.

Every *good* thing, every gift. *All of it from the Lord.*

Our home was expanding. As all the children grew, they piled in more joy and more friends. They were all fluent readers and knew their math facts. Moms ahead of me spoke of this season as the golden years, when conversation and fun fill up your days, when your children are brimming with opinions and conviction and want to understand the news and dive deep to explore the world they occupy. When our babies are little, it's hard to imagine debate; it's odd when we picture our toddler being old enough to cook or babysit or help paint a bedroom. But these years are the ones when our children creep towards maturity, and we suddenly find them friends.

I was relishing every moment. But sometimes, at crosswalks, I'd do a quick headcount and feel like we were missing someone. Nope. All there. What was that feeling that we weren't complete? Was this just more of my grief? The loss of the babies we buried would always spring up at odd times. Was that it? Or was there more? Was it that I felt there was never enough? Was this another way I wasn't satisfied with my portion, with my bread? *Lord, fill my heart with You. Help me to be content.*

When I saw two strips of blue lined up side by side on a white stick, I didn't believe it. I'd been told it wasn't even possible. After my miscarriages, my hormones ran wild and my body struggled to heal. Surgery had left me with a form of endometriosis that had, after years of complications, led my doctors to the conclusion that a hysterectomy was a wise choice for me. It was scheduled and written in ink on my calendar. But then, the test I'd had to dig for in the back of the medicine cabinet confirmed what my body had begun to tell me: I was pregnant. I cried. I didn't know if I could endure another loss. I was instantly preparing for more grief. I didn't know if I could hold hope so close and then let it go one more time. I quietly asked friends to pray. I needed the strength to carry this baby and then, I assumed, to let him or her go. This strand of my life was threadbare, frayed. I feared I would snap. I begged God to help me keep my joy. I begged Him to help me through a trial I knew might crush me. I begged Him to help me talk to my other children about what was happening and not to let their hearts become anxious. I was walking worry. I never believed I was going to hold a gift.

CHAPTER 12

Trusting the Source

Sabbath is not primarily about us or how it benefits us; it is about God, and how God forms us. It is not, in the first place, about what we do or don't do; it is about God—completing and resting and blessing and sanctifying. These are all things that we don't know much about . . . But it does mean stopping and being quiet long enough to see—open-mouthed—with wonder—resurrection wonder. . . . we cultivate the "fear of the Lord." Our souls are formed by what we cannot work up or take charge of. We respond and enter into what the resurrection of Jesus continues to do.

EUGENE PETERSON, *CHRIST PLAYS IN TEN THOUSAND PLACES*

The heartbeat whirred and whooshed on the Doppler in my doctor's office. I have always found it soothing that a womb sounds like waves on the monitor.

"Sounds strong. Size is good. Let's get another blood draw and if that looks good too, we'll see you back next week."

Her words were crisp and confident, and even though I believed the framed credentials from prestigious medical schools hanging on the office wall, I didn't trust that what she said was true. Tears began to fall down my cheeks right there. I was in a gown, in this cold room with its aqua-colored tile, sitting atop crinkly paper on the exam table. I was the picture of bare.

"Kristen, things look good." She was empathetic now, reassuring.

I wasn't biting.

"I know," I said. "I do. I've just heard that before."

It didn't matter what I did, how often I asked the Lord to fill me with faith, or how often I poured out my fears to Him. (Oh, how honestly and freely my fears were flung before Him now!) I was waiting for loss. It felt inevitable. As the weeks ticked by, I realized I might need to buy maternity clothes. *Just one pair of jeans. Don't go overboard*, I told myself. *This isn't going to last long.* Enduring was paramount. Having more babies wasn't my story. That was someone else's testimony.

Our Testimony Belongs to the Lord

In the desert while the Israelites were wandering, the Lord spoke to Moses and Aaron, telling them to take a measure of the day's manna, store it in jars, and place it before the *Testimony* of the Lord.[1] It was to be kept for all generations to remind them of the way the Lord had led them.[2] This word *testimony* is often used today to describe our own story or witness, but in the Hebrew, it means, quite literally, "the absolute solemn and divine charge." The Testimony was the Word of the Lord, the Ten Commandments, etched by his own hand onto stone. The manna was to be kept with the stone tablets in the Ark of the Covenant, a reminder of the *satisfaction* of the people and the Law. Heavenly provision and holiness were given in the manna.

Did you know that the Bible uses the word *satisfaction* when it talks about the presence of God and manna? Manna is the bread of the presence, the only thing that fills us up. This is not mere metaphor. This is our very life. This is the spiritual reality for every Christian. We are fed, we are satisfied, and we are at rest in the provision that we have no part in producing. We are made to *selah*. To pause. To meet. To stop and savor the glory of heaven on the tips of our tongues. The awe and meaning of this grace can be lost on grumbling bellies when we are forever striving to make our own days, by our own means.

How often, in my quest for control, have I wrestled the provision from my provider? I forget that feasting is for today as I furnish my plate for all possible tomorrows, and then I wonder why I have so little that hasn't spoiled. And that is exactly when I find my life contracting and getting small. When I yell or when I hide, I wonder if a practice of peace will ever become the true posture of my heart. I know I am hungry. I wonder if coming bare before the bread of the Lord's presence will ever be my first inclination. I wonder if I will keep crying over tattered pajamas when all the while, my God is preparing to clothe me with a miracle. When scarcity reigns in me like this, and I expect suffering, I'm believing the lie that that goodness will run out, that it is limited.

The Paradox of True Blessing

With every gift I've ever received, scarcity has whispered that I must stockpile. It's wise. I have to save every bit of extra for the days ahead. Scarcity misses the song that sings the story of boy with the five loaves and two fish who humbly gave his little for the Lord to make much of.[3] Scarcity cannot fathom radical generosity, the kind of life where we are made whole by the One who has been broken, where the Son of God restores us by dying for us. Christ crucified changed the economy of how we receive and how we give away.

> For whoever would save his life will lose it, but whoever loses his life for my sake will find it. For what will it profit a man if he gains the whole world and forfeits his soul?[4]

We gain our life because we lose it. When we listen to the nagging, scarcity halts our giving, justifies our neglect of the stranger, of the poor, of anyone in distress, because we can't let go of our own position of grace. It would be unwise, wouldn't it, to not care for our own bodies first? Loving my neighbor as myself, I've often heard said, means loving myself first. How easy it is to believe this when we've convinced ourselves we need to cling to our extras, but in reality we just don't want to share. I'm afraid to face the fact that in my heart, I'm often more comfortable with letting excess rot than risk giving it freely and then having it run out. I think this pattern emerges when our minds twist toward a belief that prosperity equals blessing. We become fooled into thinking that there is such a thing as destiny and all our things, our geography, our table, a full womb, and medicine to sustain us are all advantages we have been chosen for, graces given without responsibility or burden. But God has already spoken on this matter. In bold words, He has announced plainly what is favorable to Him[5]:

> Blessed are the poor in spirit, for theirs is the kingdom of heaven. Blessed are those who mourn, for they shall be comforted.

There was blessing in mourning, presence in comfort, hope in a graveyard, dependence found when I was most weak.

> Blessed are the meek, for they shall inherit the earth. Blessed are those who hunger and thirst for righteousness, for they shall be satisfied.

Hunger was a gift, it kept me running for you Lord. You fill my cup. You satisfy.

> Blessed are the merciful, for they shall receive mercy. Blessed are the pure in heart, for they shall see God.

You have been merciful to me. Gentle. Kind in my wandering, welcoming of my doubts. You have shown me Yourself, God.

> Blessed are those who are persecuted for righteousness' sake, for theirs is the kingdom of heaven. Blessed are you when others revile you and persecute you and utter all kinds of evil against you false on my account. Rejoice and be glad, for your reward is great in heaven.

You have given the kingdom of heaven to those who have suffered in your name. The reward you promise, the gifts you give are beyond compare.

Scarcity makes us beggars. But God is a giver. The maker of manna quietly whispers,

> *I am enough. I am limitless. The maker of the heavens, the vastness of oceans, the sky, of wonder. The details in a rosebud*

and a pinecone and the flavor of a strawberry all begin with Me. And if this isn't enough, I give My very self. I break My body to fill every gap, pour out My blood to fill every cup, I cover it all and beg you to eat—to be nourished and satisfied in Me alone. Your hunger was meant to be satisfied in Me. Your craving exists to point you to Me, and you have gorged yourselves on inferior bread, stored up grain to temporarily satisfy your bellies, and it has made you sick.

When we embrace our true bread, our daily bread, the fullness we find in Him has no end. It exponentially multiplies. We grow too. When we embrace Christ, we can let go of everything else because we know that what we hold is the *source* of fullness and it never, ever, ever runs out. We can give, and we can cheer, because we are full. We are whole. Scarcity lays blame on others for what we don't have; it weighs generosity with a cost; it births bitterness and feeds on contempt, incites envy and claws at personhood. I listened to its voice for far too long. Scarcity says that the world is small.

All the Good Holds Steady

When we have tasted and been filled by the Living Bread, a generosity is produced in us that opens the world up wide so that when we yield, when we confess, when we pause, when we rest, it ushers in Sabbath.

When we've wrestled in order to allow rest in our lives, it's often because we think that if we yield to it, we won't produce. We worry that we will not have enough or be enough if we stop and yield our calling, our time, our gifts. We worry that if we lay them down, we won't be able to pick them up again. And that terrifies us. What would happen if you stepped away? No, really. What would that look like?

Most of us cannot fathom a period of twenty-four hours when we are disconnected, out of touch, or unavailable. Where those who need our opinions can't ask for them right away, or where we aren't able to maintain our roles as fixers, as peacemakers—or as martyrs. We live in what has often been called the tyranny of the urgent, slave to every ping and beep coming from our electronic devices, and to all the work that will never, ever stop. Who are we, if not the person who works, who creates, who advises? Did you know that in 2015 and 2016, research showed that over half of Americans didn't take their paid vacation days?[6] Rest, freely offered, went to waste. Many workers complained that it was just too difficult to pull away, that their roles were too integral to ongoing projects, that they couldn't just quit. They might be viewed poorly if they went off to play. But they are missing the truth, which I've often forgotten too.

When I first read the parable Jesus taught about the vine and the branches in John 15:11, I skimmed over the part about what God does with good fruit:

> I am the true vine, and my Father is the gardener. He cuts off every branch in me that bears no fruit. While every branch that does bear fruit, he prunes, so that it will be even more fruitful.[7]

God not only cuts off what is dead, but prunes back what is good. He gives a rest to that which is flourishing! Because the good stuff, when it rests, when it is pruned back and not overloaded will then become *more* fruitful. We don't have to live in a mindset that tempts us to believe that fruit will fade if we exercise restraint. All the good stuff holds steady.

Rest and Provision

God's voice always sings true. The cherubim and seraphim will always bow; He must and will always be the object of praise, and even the rocks will cry out to proclaim His holiness if man does not. His Word will always carry weight, true and sure. When He establishes rest, it is our joy to embrace it. When the Lord established Sabbath with His people, one day out of seven was to rest and not labor. In one year out of seven, there was to be a solemn rest for the land where all growing stopped. The land was to lie fallow. Leviticus 25:6 says, "the Sabbath of the land shall provide food for you."[8] It took me a moment to catch that. The Sabbath shall provide food! All their hunger would be met by their rest. Rest and provision were inextricably linked. Intertwined. One produced the other. Farmers today often let a field lie fallow so that it can produce again and not grow weary. When the land rests, it receives an infusion of carbon and nitrogen that allows it to produce well for several years afterward. This is exactly what God prescribed for the land of Israel and also what He prescribes for us, for the refreshment of our souls.

Then, in the fiftieth year, there was to be a jubilee. It's almost impossible to picture. During the jubilee, the special Sabbath year, liberty was to be proclaimed. All property was to be returned to the original holder of deeds, debts were to be forgiven, bond slaves were to be freed. This was to be a year of social justice enacted and preserved for the people, of ecological rest for the land. It was a system that simply required obedience to yield and celebrate. And yet God's people could not be still. Their actions proved they did not trust the source of all good things.

Biblical scholars tell us there never was a jubilee. There was never even a seventh-year rest in Israel. The people kept striving to produce food themselves, afraid that if they stopped, they might starve. Oh, how I recognize myself in their fear. The act of yielding, of ceasing, is an act of trust. It is a proclamation of your own heart, before the Lord, before the watching world, that you trust that you will have enough because none of it is dependent upon *you*. When we rest, we proclaim that we have a provider who *is* our rest.

When we see the Israelites carried off to Babylon approximately five hundred years later, the land they inhabited lay vacant for seventy years in their absence. If you do the math, there were about five hundred years between the time of Moses and the Babylonian exile. Seventy Sabbath years. Exactly the number forgotten since the commandment had been given. God's Word was set. His heart was clear.

> All the time that it lies desolate, the land will have the rest it did not have during the Sabbaths you lived in it . . . I will remember my covenant with Jacob and my covenant with Isaac and my covenant with Abraham, and I will remember the land. For the land will be deserted by them and will enjoy its Sabbaths while it lies desolate without them. They will pay for their sins because they rejected my laws and abhorred my decrees. But for their sake I will remember the covenant with their ancestors whom I brought out of Egypt in the sight of the nations to be their God. I am the LORD.[9]

Rest mattered. The bent of our marrow is to always forget. *But He will not forget.* Lord help my unbelief.

The phone rang, and I ran to grab it before it went to voicemail. I was an expert at leaping across my bed and onto the other side, but this time as I flopped, I caught myself and eased my way across. My belly was round now and prevented my sloppy slide-and-reach for the phone on the nightstand. I still wasn't accustomed to my changing shape. The phone rang again.

"Hello?"

My doctor was calling today. This had to be her. She wanted to personally tell me the results of various tests. She was tender; she knew I was fearing another loss.

"Kristen, the baby looks wonderful. And I know you did want to find out, correct? Well, you are having a little boy. A little boy!"

She'd said it twice for emphasis. A little boy.

"Congratulations!"

Her words hung in the air, as I imagined the face of my son for the first time. I pictured his little nose and lips, the wiggle of his toes. I pictured nursing him, holding his tiny fingers in my palm, swaddling his tiny body and rocking him back and forth. I'd been afraid to buy baby clothes. I wanted to hold on to the worry of my heart more than I wanted to rent it out to hope and a future. But rest had come for me too, and not in a way I had ever expected. My ultrasound had shown that I had placenta previa, a condition that, for me, meant complete bedrest. New York is a walking city—there was rarely a day when I didn't reach 10,000 steps on my fitness tracker. Bedrest meant isolation. Silence. As a familiar fear crept in and lurked, I was reminded of those early days and months as a new mother finding the promise of stillness in the practice of honest and raw prayer. *Lord, am I really doing this again? Really this time?*

There was never any idea that another baby could replace the girls we had lost, but there was a whisper of a different gift, something new, spoken in the words of my doctor and in the peace that began to warm me in the room where I sat reflecting. A demarcation—a setting apart—of a child. A boy. A son. A new promise.

As the months of my pregnancy wore on, friends pitched in in the sweetest ways. We were surrounded by help, by company and so much love. And I, in a state of forced immobility, learned how to embrace being still once again. This time it may have been imposed upon me, but I knew its worth. I was resting not just in the coolness of my comforters or in my leather chair, I was exhaling deep from my soul to God. And I kept living in the wait. I camped out in the in-between and the unknown. It was the safest place to be. It was where my fears collided with the person who was *selah* incarnate. And He held me there, reshaping my whole world.

CHAPTER 13

Where Peace Fills

Pure "Northernness" engulfed me; a vision of huge clear spaces hanging above . . . in the endless twilight of Northern summer, remoteness, severity . . . And almost at the same moment I knew that I had met this before, long, long ago . . . And with that plunge back into my own past, there arose at once, almost like heartbreak, the memory of Joy itself, the knowledge that I had once had what I had now lacked for years, that I was returning at last from exile and desert lands to my own country, and the distance of my own past Joy, both unattainable, flowed together in a single, unendurable sense of desire and loss.

C.S. LEWIS, *SURPRISED BY JOY*

We're up early, just the two of us, my baby boy and me, on a Sunday. We peek through the glass and watch the grey-white shards of branches dancing in the line of trees above the street. Their limbs are bare now, bumpy and cold, expecting frost. Fog is gathering in rolls down the hill. It inches through the bushes in swaths of white and grey. The sky is just now brightening as the sun rises. I'm still getting used to the green of Oregon, the new wild of the north, the landscape of our returning. Moss covers the tree just beyond my window, lacing delicately all the way down to the ivy that lines the wall of the kitchen. Bold green surfacing in a sea of grey fog. It's odd to see the green trail along rough bark instead of the smooth stone I was accustomed to seeing in Manhattan. Weather in the city looked different somehow. I look down at tiny fingers stretching into my own as my baby boy arches his back, learning how his muscles move and becoming aware of the world he is waking to.

For us, new life coincided with a conclusion. Josh's company gave him an invitation to a new kind of work on the West Coast. It was another one of those opportunities we knew God was nudging us to follow. The paradox of a beginning and an ending met in the life of a baby felt profound.

We named him Harris. He carries the legacy of his grandfather with him, the memory of a man who shaped Josh's love of adventure and nature trails and travel. He had a heart for exploration, and to us, he embodied the spirit of the West and the idea of moving in faith.

As this boy and I take in the colors of early morning, I can't stop looking at him. I still can't believe I'm holding such hope. Did Mary feel like this too, when she held the hope of the world in her arms? When she nursed Him? Cradled Him?

The first time I knew Jesus was real, that He had come to Earth as a baby, was in my basement during the week of Epiphany. Candlelight was our only guide as we filed down the hall. My fingers were pressed into the hands of my little sister, squeezing her along as we bumped between the other children. An adult voice whispered.

Everyday objects and photographs mounted on the wall looked fuzzy in the darkness. For a moment I let my mind imagine that we'd been transported, that we were no longer on a typical American street on a slushy winter evening but in Bethlehem. We were looking for Him—for baby Jesus, the Messiah born in a manger. And as we approached a new light in the distance, we were invited to sit with the shepherd as he told us the story of chasing the star and meeting the new baby king.

It was really just my father in his old red bathrobe. The same one he wore as he shaved his face every morning, coating it in white cream and sliding his razor down his cheeks and chin line by line. But there, in that moment, the red robe looked regal, ancient. The hood was up, covering his black mop of hair, transforming him. It was anything but mundane as he whispered to us the glory of seeing the Christ child fresh and new.

I didn't realize then how rare my childhood was—all the parents at our little parish cultivated ways to *show* Jesus to their children. I can remember Mrs. Govcia in the fourth grade saying, "Don't just tell me, Kristi, show me with your words. You are a writer!" She knew the secret, and my parents did too, that all our fondest memories would be wrapped up in stories we could see and taste and touch. All our celebrations did this too. They pointed to Jesus. They didn't just tell me, they *showed* me wonder and majesty.

Feasts and Stones to Remember

They showed me all year long. When the skies were a brittle blue in autumn and smoke curled toward heaven, leaving the earthy smell of burn piles below, I knew it was nearly time to sleep under the sukkah. The seventh feast of the year, the feast of Tabernacles or Sukkot, is when the Jewish people celebrate a time of dwelling and fellowship with the Lord. With a keen eye for how to make Scripture come alive, my parents and their friends created a day to remember this festival in our own way at harvest time. God had instructed the Israelites to make crude houses to remember their years of living in tents in the desert, simple shelters to remember the years when He fed them with manna.

Our family tradition while I was growing up was to remember how God came to dwell among His people, and how He was dwelling with us still in Christ. The fathers and children built sukkahs with plywood and saws and hammers all pounding. The mothers would drape fabric over the top, and on all sides boughs of trees, gourds, and leaves were all tucked in. We prepared for a day of feasting together, calling it the *Festival of the Booths*. Children bobbed for apples and bounced from booth to booth carving pumpkins, painting faces, decorating cookies, making candles, and pressing cider.

For weeks beforehand, my mother worked on our banner of felt and fabric, sewing seam by seam. My favorite was the flag with all the fruits of the Spirit sewn on with gold thread. Like the tribes in the wilderness, each family would march through the orchard and down to the water, carrying our banners, marks of who we served and belonged to and all He had poured into us. My sister and I carried our banner with my mother and father, lined up with all our friends as we made our way to the sukkahs together, singing in a chorus as loud as we could, "He brought me to his banqueting table . . . His banner over me is love."

When I think of the standard of God, of His love, of his covering, how He dwells with us, I remember those crisp nights building the sukkah. I remember the singing, the cider, the cookies, the bonfire in the early evening. The warmth of those celebrations, hidden in my heart, rise and brighten today.

Those golden days brought delight to our hearts as children, but they also spoke truth to our souls. They soaked in deep so that as we grew and encountered dry deserts and seasons of desperate hunger, we would remember that we served a God who is with us and who builds beauty in barren places. Interludes of beauty, of feasting were created by God to remind us all of what we are prone to forget. In the spring, the Passover Seder sees the suffering servant, the Christ, pierced in the lines that run through the matzah bread. The bitter herbs remind each generation of the sour years from which the Israelites were freed. The lamb, remembered for its blood spread over every doorframe, causing the angel of death to "pass over" and spare their firstborn, foreshadows the Lamb of God, His firstborn and only Son, killed in our place. And the Eucharist, Communion, the holy meal of the Last Supper reminds us whenever we gather that we are fed and sustained by the wine and the bread, the blood and body of Jesus.

One of my own family's traditions is to create a stone of remembrance from time to time. When we finish a season, a school year, or a summer vacation full of memories; when we experience a joy, a loss, or come out of a trying time; we mark it, note it and make sure it becomes a part of our family story. This idea is modeled after the Israelites in Joshua 4. Before they entered the Promised Land, they first had to pass over the Jordan River, and it wasn't merely a shallow wade.

The Lord commanded the priests to carry the Ark of the Covenant, where the Lord Himself was dwelling, into the water ahead of the people. It was a miracle akin to the parting of the Red Sea. He was going to part a way for them and promised:

> When the soles of the feet of the priest bearing the ark of the LORD, the Lord of all the earth, shall rest in the waters of the Jordan, the waters of the Jordan shall be cut off from flowing, and the waters coming down from above shall stand in one heap.[1]

And then, when the whole nation had passed through the water, a man from each of the twelve tribes was instructed to take a stone from before the ark as a sign among them so that, as the Lord told them,

> When your children ask in time to come, "What do these stones mean to you?" then you shall tell them that the waters of the Jordan were cut off before the ark of the covenant of the LORD. When it passed over the Jordan, the waters of the Jordan were cut off. So these stones shall be to the people of Israel a memorial forever.[2]

The stones were their testimony of all God had done and of His very presence with them. When people ask us about crossing the country to move twice, even when my children question why we moved and moved again, I want the answer that is ready on my lips to echo the words of the Israelites to their own children when they asked about the special stones of remembrance and how they crossed the Jordan:

> So that all the peoples of the earth may know that the hand of the LORD is mighty, that you may fear the LORD your God forever.[3]

As our time to leave New York drew near, we prepared our apartment for moving vans to come and spent the last week riding around in cabs to say farewell to all our old haunts. At each place, we talked about our favorite memories there, listed the gifts it had given us. We took photos and sketched pictures and wrote in our journals about what God had done, until the last night when we walked across the street to Central Park. One by one friends came to say goodbye, embracing us, until we we'd become a flock, chatting and laughing while the children all played in the fountains and swung together on the playground, racing down the slides like they had on so many other afternoons. But this one was different. As I looked at each face, felt each hug, reflected on each moment and all the ways God had shown me His delight and beauty in this city, I realized it had changed me forever. I would be forever marked by my life in Manhattan, formed and shaped in the contours of my soul because of how God met me there. The goodbyes lingered past sunset, and as we walked home for the last time, past Billy's hotdog cart, past our doorman, we knew this night was distinctive, worthy of being set apart with a stone.

Selah and Sabbath Shows Us How

When the priests were told to stand in the Jordan River and bring the ark of the covenant to rest, the Lord cut the waters, and Scripture says he rested there. Essentially, the Lord waded out first, and by His very presence made a way. When we practice peace, it is always about embracing the rest God provides. He always goes first. Into waters, into suffering, into new lands, into great joy, into glory, and into rest—there is nothing He gives without giving thoroughly of Himself.

The Sabbath encompasses all our rhythms as its liturgy flows and gives form to the week ahead, to begin with rest in us, to begin in Him. To be fed, to be reminded, and to be renewed. Sabbath is the *selah* of our week, where earth meets heaven and where, in between, as we come, we proclaim together that His kingdom is truer and more real than the one of this earth.

Do you see yet that *selah* is the meeting place of great exchange? That it is how God gives? It's how He pours out peace, delights us with beauty, and bestows Himself on us. In yielding, stopping, and choosing to trust, we are not limited; these are practices that free, disciplines that allow us to enter a life shaped by the world of heaven. That is the secret of Sabbath living. Sabbath reveals the kingdom come. God with us. We pause in pews and take our place in line for bread; we worship. But Sabbath is not about what we bring—Sabbath is about what God gives. It is our one day in seven to feast on manna, the bread of the presence. It is His presence that cut off waters, that hung on a cross, that dwelt and still dwells with His people, *in* His people. It is His presence that satisfies us and bars our wanting anything less. Sabbath carries an order of holiness that brings hope in reminding us of who we are as bearers of light. Sabbath transforms us because in it, we are met. Sabbath is the place where we reunite with our Father on the road and leap into His arms, knowing that in that meeting we will be transformed. In Sabbath we remember the embrace. Even the order of liturgy in our churches mirrors a pattern of prayer and relationship with God that spins into the rest of our week. First we adore and we praise, then we confess, relinquishing our burdens vulnerably and wholly, and seeking forgiveness for our sins before embracing God's gifts with thanks and affirming His love with thanksgiving.

Scenes from a Sunday

Selah takes shape when I wake in the morning light with Harry. Every week on Sunday, I rise expectant. I nurse in the big chair and know my coffee is waiting: espresso shots pulled and poured over with steamed milk, cinnamon sprinkled gently across the foam. Today I'll scramble eggs. I'm craving a savory flavor, tomatoes and basil with sea salt. Sometimes it's toast and cheese, sometimes a Belgian waffle. Maia is now thirteen and loves to join me in the kitchen or cook a feast for us herself. Jones wakes before we are done. My two early birds greet me and help plan delight. Always delight on the Lord's day.

We'll wake the others soon, get dressed for church, pour tea, braid hair. We'll slide into the warm seats of our car and drive to church. We'll sing and pray and remember aloud; we'll confess. We'll eat the bread and drink the wine. We'll give thanks. When we come home, we often keep resting and reading. We stretch into naps and play board games. Some afternoons we venture to the ocean or a local park. We'll leave the dishes and the piles of clothes because we know our work will be there tomorrow, that the heart of this day means that filling our souls with heaven matters more than living forever tidy.

Our rhythms are all becoming worn, the ins and outs of large family living keep us ever swaying. The pace and bustle outside my door and in my own heart always leans toward becoming too busy and too much. These days of going intentionally and slowly, of finding ways to yield our time—to stop stockpiling and surrender—bring an ease to each of us.

Later this week I will try to run for the first time since childbirth. I'm itching to take in the pond in case the forecast indeed lays snow and ice like blankets throughout the city. When it begins I'll watch the flakes fall and sip hot tea from my perch next to the fire, in front of the big picture window. I know my girls will need to slip Harris into my arms the moment I return; we haven't mastered mama leaving his side for long. The snowy months ahead will be defined by the curve of his body in my arms, close and secure. My older children will snuggle near me with their books and schoolwork, and we'll talk about their thoughts and ideas. I've been waiting for frustrations over converting fractions to explode for a while now, and I think the assignments this week may just be the tipping point.

But as the storm comes, I will remind them in the comfort of the den that rest must be inserted right into the line-up of our days. Sunday to Sunday, *selah* becomes our daily invitation. *Selah* is the practice we are given between two worlds, this one and the next, to remember this gift of peace. It is a practice, an ongoing work, and we set about it imperfectly. But its constancy is sure. *Selah* is here. It is among us. We need only stretch open hands and receive.

Because after all, it's not about what we bring. It's about what God *gives.*

We will welcome the storm when it comes alongside all the details and tasks, and we will stop to run outside and catch snow on our tongues and eyelashes. We will wonder aloud if it looks anything like the manna that fell.

Acknowledgments

It has been an incredible source of joy to pour my heart into these pages. When it comes to writing these acknowledgments, I've found myself wanting to thank every single person I've ever met who has inspired, encouraged, or equipped me for this work, including past librarians and the mailman who helped me with the postage for my first query letter to a magazine in fifth grade. However, there are a few who have made an indelible mark not only upon my life, but in a practical way that is essential to the production of the words you now hold:

Thank you first off to Stephanie Smith, my brilliant editor, who saw the potential of this project from the beginning and spoke life into its form from our very first meeting. Your vision and depth of insight shaped not only this work, but my heart. I will be forever grateful for the care you have given to me and to these words, especially when I didn't know if I had it in me to finish. I am so honored to have been inspired, challenged, and spurred on by you. You know I really do think you are a genius. Thank you to others who invested in this message as well: Harmony Harkema, Brandon Henderson, Robin Barnett, Estee Zandee, and the entire team at Zondervan, for your commitment to me and this project. I am humbled to be counted among your community of authors. You are truly are a dream team.

To my agent, Don Jacobson, his wife Brenda, and everyone at DC Jacobson Literary Agency (Marty, Blair, and Laurel), thank you for your belief in me, for your constant support and prayer, for helping me to develop this narrative in its earliest drafts, and for shepherding the entire process. Your wisdom and counsel are a blessing to me, and our friendship means the most of all.

To Sally Clarkson, my mentor, my friend, and my podcasting partner, you have taught me so much about home, ministry, writing, and God's heart for me. Working with you, laughing with you, and learning from you is all grace. Thank you for the trust you have placed in me, for allowing me to become a part of Whole Heart Ministries, and for your constant care of my soul. Let's eat chocolate and talk about ideas forever.

To my precious writing group: Logan Wolfram, Kat Lee, Chrystal Evans Hurst, Sarah Mae Hoover, and Jamie Ivey: You have walked with me through every single step of the writing process, and without your constant counsel, insight, and laughter, I may have quite literally been unable to write this book.

To friends a who have cheered for me along the way and whose lives sharpen me always: Sara Hagerty, Karen Stott, Ruth Simons, Ruth Schwenk, Kari Jo Cates, Chris Whitford, Margaret Kramer, Emily Salz, Heather Dufek, Laurie Black, Amanda Walters, Rita Abruzzi, Nika Buckley Shawna Sullivan, Lauren Smith, Ginger Vassar, and the entire national team of dear friends at Mom Heart. To the members of West Side Women and Thursday Moms' group, and the entire community of Redeemer's W83 in New York City: I am forever changed by the rhythms of grace we shared together, our time pondering Scripture, and for every afternoon spent at Hippo or Wild West. Thanks as well to all our neighbors who made NYC home, and for allowing some of your stories to be shared here.

To John and Laura Waldren, my dad and mom: your influence

and heritage is all over these pages. Thank you for a childhood steeped in wonder and in God's Word. You have given me an eternal gift in your unending love and parenting. To Jim and Shelly Kill, my incredible in-laws, thank you for your encouragement and all the grandparent dates that occupied my kids on long writing weekends. Thank you Julie and Ryan, Heath and Elisa, and Sasha and Ryan for being such steady companions and friends as well as the very best brothers and sisters. GG and Art, thank you for your constant encouragement and for sharing your joy with me every time we are together. To the entire Trimble Tribe, my anchor: our family legacy is beloved to me, as are all our group text messages, prayers, memories and every moment when we are all together. Auntie Ginny, thank you for all your comments on early drafts; your kindness made it easier to take these words outside of my journal. Thank you, too, Auntie Sue and Uncle Dean for the weeks of rest and retreat you have given us at the cabin, where my soul was able to breathe and where so much of this book was written.

And finally to my most beloved people in the all the world: Josh, you have walked this story with me and carried it in your heart too. Thank you for being faithful to ceaselessly point me to Jesus. Thank you for encouraging me to write always, for bearing more than your share of everything at home in this intense season of publishing, and for seeing the value of work in my life. Whenever I want to quit, you help me press onward and inspire me to be more excellent. Halle, Maia, Jones, and Lael, thank you for sharing me while I spent so many afternoons in front of my computer screen. Your excitement about this project, the treats you brought into my office, and all your encouragement and pride were treasured in the process of writing this book. And to

Harris, whose early months were shaped by sleeping beside me as I wrote, your presence brought sheer delight and harnessed my focus in the best way possible. Our family is the most important work of my life, and being with you is my greatest joy and my favorite place. I love you forever.

Notes

Chapter 1: From Silence to Symphony

1. Eugene Peterson. *Psalms: Prayers for the Heart-12 Studies for Individuals or Groups* (Downer's Grove: Intervarsity Press), 1987, 2000.
2. Psalm 46:10
3. Exodus 14:13
4. Psalm 65:7–8

Chapter 2: The Hardest Part

1. Oxford English Dictionary www.oed.com
2. Mark 3:4 ESV
3. Hebrews 1:1–4
4. CSB
5. Job 30:20–23
6. ESV
7. Psalm 91
8. Joseph Benson. *Commentary of the Old and New Testament* (New York; T. Carlton and J Porter, 1857).
9. Psalm 33:6
10. C. S. Lewis. *The Magician's Nephew* (London: Harper Collins, 2014).

Chapter 3: To Leave Between

1. ESV
2. ESV
3. ESV

Chapter 5: A Curve in the Road

1. Psalm 33:6

Chapter 7: How His Music Heals

1. http://www.stlouischildrens.org/articles/features/2014/music-therapy-helps-infants-in-the-newborn-intensive-care-unit-nicu.
2. Ibid.
3. 1 Corinthians 14:26
4. Ephesians 5:19 NASB
5. Proverbs 31: 25–26 ESV
6. Letters of St. Jerome
7. Psalm 98
8. Psalm 90
9. John 1:1–5
10. Dietrich Bonhoeffer. *Life Together: The Classic Exploration of Christian Community* (New York: Harper and Row, 1954).
11. Ibid.

Chapter 8: Practicing Selah

1. Luke 1:38 ESV
2. Luke 1:46–55 ESV

Chapter 9: When We Miss Eden

1. C.S. Lewis. *The Weight of Glory* (London: William Collins, 2013).
2. Ezekiel 37
3. Psalm 34:8
4. 1 Corinthians 5:8
5. Leslie Newbigin. *Gospel in a Pluralist Society* (Grand Rapids: Wm. B. Eerdmans Publishing Co., 1989).
6. Julian Barnes, "Nothing to Be Afraid Of," *The New York Times*; October 3, 2008.
   http://www.nytimes.com/2008/10/05/books/chapters/chap-nothing-to-be-frightened-of.html
7. C. S. Lewis. *The Lion, The Witch, and the Wardrobe* (London: Harper Collins, 2014).
8. 2 Peter 1:19 CSB

Chapter 10: Eyes to See

1. Matthew 6:22
2. Acts 9:1
3. Exodus 34:29–30
4. Exodus 16:4–7 ESV
5. Exodus 24:16, 40:34
6. John 1:14 ESV
7. Matthew 17:2
8. Hebrews 1:3
9. John 17:1
10. Matthew 27:49, paraphrased
11. Romans 1:21–25

Chapter 11: When We Fear Scarcity

1. Matthew 13:24–30 ESV
2. Eyfan Bachar, Laura Canetti, Elliot M. Berry, "Lack of Longlasting Consequences of Starvation on Eating Pathology in Jewish Holocaust Survivors of Nazi Concentration Camps," *Journal of Abnormal Psychology*, Vol. 114 (1), February 2005, 165–169. DOI: 10.1037/0021–843X.114.165.
3. John 6:48–51 ESV

Chapter 12: Trusting the Source

1. Exodus 16:33–34 KJV
2. See Deuteronomy 8
3. Luke 9:16
4. Matthew 16:25–26 ESV
5. Matthew 5 ESV
6. http://money.cnn.com/2016/12/19/pf/employees-unused-paid-vacation-days/.
7. ESV
8. ESV
9. Leviticus 26:43–45 ESV

Chapter 13: Where Peace Fills

1. Joshua 3:13 ESV
2. Joshua 4:6–7 ESV
3. Joshua 4:24 ESV